NAVY-WIDE EXA
ADVANCEMEN
FOR E-4 TH

D0292401

A consolidation of two books formerly titled:
"Navy-Wide Examination Advancement Guide for E-3/4/5" &
"Navy-Wide Examination Advancement Guide for E-6/7"

Copyright© 1986, 2000 by Harlan E. Flick
Updated   2007

For information, address:
Professional Management Spectrum, Inc.
PO Box 30330
Pensacola, Florida 32503
www.servicebooks.com

ISBN: 1-879123-05-3

The words "he, "him," and "his" in this Guide are used to communicate ideas, and are not intended to discriminate against anyone.

PRINTED IN THE UNITED STATES OF AMERICA

APRIL BREAREY

FORWARD

In today's highly technical Navy, an enlisted person is generously afforded the opportunity to progress up the chain of command as a reward for superior performance and proper military bearing. However, the largest stepping-stone in this progression is usually one major obstacle - an examination. The enlisted sailor must first pass an examination prior to being advanced or being determined as "selection board eligible."

I believe that there is **no reason** why an average sailor cannot pass any advancement examination that the Navy administers. People **can be taught** to obtain better scores on examinations.

This guide was prepared through my own experiences of preparing myself and my subordinates for exams during my Navy career. It conveys innovative rules, practices, and attitudes that have proven themselves successful time and time again.

Because you have chosen this guide, I know that you are ready for the success you deserve.

Good luck.

Harlan E. Flick

NAVY-WIDE EXAMINATION ADVANCEMENT GUIDE FOR E-4 Thru E-7

TABLE OF CONTENTS

CHAPTER ONE

ADVANCEMENT

Why don't people get advanced when they are eligible to assume the responsibility and gain the additional monetary benefits? Every year we find a large percentage of eligible personnel not competing for advancement. Or they don't get advanced when they do compete. This is due to two main causes: (1) there aren't enough people interested in going up for an advancement in rate; or, (2) they aren't receiving a high enough final multiple score on the exams in order to be advanced.

STAY NON-RATED?

Let's discuss number (1) from above for a minute. There are a lot of happy E-3s out there! That fact is hard to believe for many of us, but many young men and women today would rather stay non-rated for their entire tour in the military just to be more free of responsibilities and not get "bogged down" with studies and preparations for advancement. They would rather take liberty time than the extra hours that may be required in completing Personnel Advancement Requirements (PARS). They probably couldn't be bothered with filling out military and professional correspondence courses. Maybe they feared the performance test that may have been a requirement prior to going up for rate. It always makes me wonder what these people tell prospective employers after their military stint is over. Probably something like, "I only made it to E-3, but I was a darn good one." Did you ever overhear someone in casual conversation back home jokingly blurt out, "When I was in the Navy, I got advanced all the way to Seaman!" That person may be laughing on the outside, but, believe me, he's probably crying a little on the inside. If you are reading this, you probably are not among those personnel in category (1). But look around your ship or station, and you can spot plenty of these "career non-rates."

FINAL MULTIPLE

There is a chance that you may be, or could later fall into category (2). Plenty of people miss being advanced during every Navy-wide examination cycle because of the score they received on the required exam. Most of the lower scores are due to lack of study or poor preparation practices. Another major reason is that they do not have enough practical knowledge about taking multiple-choice exams. It is not difficult to pass any Navy-wide examination. Over 90% of the candidates that take every exam pass it. The problem is obtaining the required Final Multiple Score (FMS) to become advanced. The FMS is the exam score combined with points given for length of service, performance marks, time in pay-grade, awards, and previous "passed-but-not-advanced" scores. As you can see, the points allowed in the FMS other than the exam score can take an extraordinary amount of time to grow. Most of these factors employ "time" and "performance" barriers, and the easiest of all the factors to increase the FMS is the exam factor. The higher the exam score, the higher the FMS.

MULTIPLE COMPUTATION

The following table contains an example breakdown of the areas considered in computing the final multiple score for advancement competition. As you can see, the performance that you exhibit on the examination is a priority that cannot be overlooked.

ADVANCEMENT MULTIPLE COMPUTATION

AREA	E-4/5	E-6	E-7
Rating Examinations	34%	30%	60%
Evaluations	36%	41.5%	40%
Service in Pay Grade	13%	13%	-----
Awards	4 %	4.5%	-----
"PNA" Points	13%	11%	-----

WHAT DO YOU NEED TO PASS?
Everyone is interested in what is required of them prior to going into a test. Here's what the Navy requires.

First, we must distinguish between "standard" and "raw" scores. Standard scores are based on the highest possible score of 80. The raw score is the actual number of questions answered correctly on an exam. You never actually "see" this number on your profile sheet after the exam is graded. Each rating exam has 200 questions. Each of these 200 questions is worth a percentage in determining your standard score. The standard score is decided after all exams for your rating are graded, and then marked on a "curve," so that the highest scoring individual(s) receive the 80 (highest) standard score points, the second highest receives the 79 standard score points, and so on.

AN "ACE?"

It is all but impossible to "ace" any Navy-wide exam. It is a common misconception throughout the fleet to assume an "80" standard score is an "ace" on the exam. Not true. It actually means that that person was in the group with the highest Navy-wide score. This is truly something to be proud of, but it could mean that the candidate had a total of 120 out of 150 questions correct.

RAW SCORE

The raw score is the actual number of questions you had correct on the exam. The raw score is compared to all others who took the exam, and the standard score is derived after the averaging occurs. Remember, it is the standard score, not the raw score that gets applied toward the final multiple calculation.

ADVANCEMENT TO PAYGRADES E-4 THROUGH E-7

The Advancement Manual provides us the process by which individuals can advance to paygrades E-4 through E-9. Advancement is obtained by competition in a Navywide Advancement In-Rate Examination. Exams are given according to a set schedule at pre-arranged locations and times announced in advance.

The Exams have 200 questions, and some questions on each exam will be based on occupational standards and a portion of the questions will be dedicated to professional military knowledge. Here are the ratios of question dedication on each pay-grade examination

RATIO OF QUESTIONS

Pay Grade	Occupational Stds	Military Knowledge
E-4	150	50
E-5	135	65
E-6	115	85
E-7	100	100

ADVANCEMENT BENEFITS

Along with advancement in the Navy come such things as better pay, more interesting and challenging job assignments, greater respect from your shipmates, and the self-satisfaction of progressing up the career ladder of your chosen occupational field.

PREREQUISITES

Besides the examination, what else has to be done in order to get advanced in the Navy? The answer to this question is in several steps that must be completed. This takes a certain amount of planning and coordination of time and performance on your part. Below you will find a listing of items that must be completed prior to the examination date. Some of these may or may not apply to you, depending on the rating you are in. The best verification of your requirements is through your Education Services Office.

REQUIREMENTS PRIOR TO EXAM

COMMANDING OFFICER'S RECOMMENDATION

This is the most important requirement. The CO's recommendation is what starts the advancement process rolling. The recommendation must be documented in your enlisted evaluation. Once a commanding officer recommends you for advancement, it remains valid until it is withdrawn. The recommendation remains valid if you are transferred to another command.

PERFORMANCE MARK

For advancement to E-4 through E-6, you must have at least the minimum overall performance mark average required (whatever the standard may be at the time). See current edition of the Advancement Manual, or check with ESO office.

PROPER PATH OF ADVANCEMENT

This basically means that you must stay within your proper occupational field. For instance, you could not go up for Third Class Gunners Mate if you were a Fireman, or you could not take a Boatswains Mate test if you were a Hospitalman.

MILITARY REQUIREMENTS/ STANDARDS

With the Navy-Wide Military Leadership exams no longer being produced, military questions will be placed on the Navy-Wide exams, incorporated along with questions concerning your rating. The questions will be based on military standards, with an increased emphasis on military requirements knowledge.

This means that leadership questions will directly affect your final multiple from the exam! This also means that the back part of this book is more important to you now than ever before!

NAVY TRAINING COURSE
This may not apply to you at the Third Class level if you are a graduate of an "A" School. It can be substituted by several methods, depending upon your rating and command policy. Whatever the requirement in your case, it should be completed one month prior to the Navy-wide advancement exam. The Rate Training Course is never a bad idea, so it is highly recommended that you complete it, no matter what the standard requirement is.

SERVICE SCHOOL
Some ratings require that you attend a school prior to entry into that specific rating. This only applies to a few occupational ratings, but the best thing to do is check with your career counselor before you start working toward one of them.

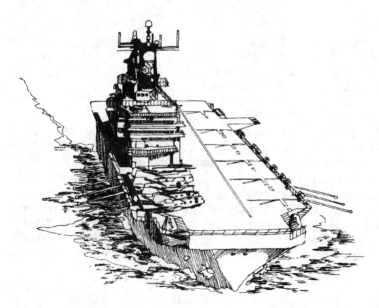

PAR

Personnel Advancement Requirements (PAR) is a check-off list for each pay grade within a rating. It is presented in three sections: Section I lists various administrative requirements (such as time-in-rate, etc.). Section II lists formal schools or other training required for each pay grade. Section III lists occupational and military ability requirements. The ability requirements are broad statements of what a person must be able to do in the next higher pay grade. PAR is applicable to E-4 through E-7 candidates, and should be completed one month prior to the Navy-wide advancement exam. Once again, check Page 4 of your service record to make sure these are entered as "completed."

TIME IN RATE

The minimum time in rate requirements for each pay grade are as listed below:

Pay Grade	Time in Previous Pay Grade
E-4	6 months as E-3
E-5	12 months as E-4
E-6	36 months as E-5
E-7	36 months as E-6
E-8	36 months as E-7
E-9	36 months as E-8

PHYSICALLY QUALIFIED

Special physical requirements for some ratings exist. The Manual of Navy Enlisted Manpower and Personnel Classifications and Occupational Standards (NAVPERS 18068) can tell you exactly what they are. As a general rule, those who exceed the weight and body fat percentage standards may take the exam for advancement if all other requirements have been met. However, the commanding officer can withhold the actual advancement of those who do not show satisfactory progress in that area.

PASS NAVY-WIDE RATING EXAM

Here is where you have the chance to really show your stuff! Refer back to the multiple computation table a few pages back, and you can readily see how important this exam can be. Raise that final multiple score by learning how to prepare for and take Navy multiple-choice exams!

WHO GETS ADVANCED?

The people who get advanced are the ones who have properly prepared themselves for exam day. They spend the extra time completing all the prerequisites, and obviously study to prepare for the rating exam. They complete their Personnel Qualifications in plenty of time, act in a professional manner, obtaining evaluation marks within range of recommendation for advancement, and complete all require correspondence courses.

MEET THE TEST PREPARED

Meeting the test prepared, and "beating" it, has become one of the essential arts of success in America today. This is a fact especially evident to Navy personnel. Many people think that they took their last examination on the day they completed school. Not so. A person takes and has a requirement to pass examinations in almost every walk of life. Test taking is an art that can be learned, just like any other art. Successful practice of this art is a talent which must be exercised in order to progress in a Naval career. This need of mastering tests will not end in the military. Even corporate giants such as General Motors and General Electric utilize tests at all levels of employment. There are also licensing tests in all major trades, such as contractors, plumbers, and electricians. You must view any **test** you take in the Navy as a **conTEST**. You are competing against others for advancement. Your score must be higher than a certain number of individuals that take the same examination in order for you to be advanced.

YOU CAN BE TAUGHT TO IMPROVE TEST-TAKING
It is a total misconception to believe that a person cannot be taught to improve his performance on examinations. If you use the information provided in this guide, and apply the principles within, you will, without doubt, improve your testing skill on exam days. This useful information will not only assist you in answering test items on information that you know. You will also gain knowledge in techniques of how to answer those questions that you do not know, or are not completely sure of.

CHAPTER TWO

EXAMINATION DEVELOPMENT

Navy-wide exams are developed by senior (E-7 through E-9) personnel in your occupational rating. Many people have believed in the past that the exams are computer-generated from a long list or "bank" of questions stored in some large machine, and conveniently "spit out" just prior to the distribution of each examination. Not so. Exam construction is a long and totally human process. It is a process accomplished very similar to the way a person should study. Research is done by reviewing Rate Training Manuals, technical and administrative publications, specific Naval Warfare Publications, and several other references that apply to a specific rating. Items are "highlighted" from these references for use in the examination process. If you know a little more about what your exam writer does, it should help you in studying for exams.

WHAT THEY DO

Each rating in the Navy has at least two representatives stationed at the Naval Education and Training Professional Development & Technology Center in Pensacola, Florida. One of these is the Rate Training Manual/Correspondence Course writer, and the other person develops the examinations. They work closely together in researching references and developing items for inclusion in either the courses or the exams. The exam writer keeps abreast of what the rate training manual writer places in the updated manuals, so that he can concurrently update the exam items.

The writers work as a team with a civilian education specialist in the development of their materials. The writers provide the technical knowledge necessary, while the education specialist provides the proper format and testing criteria. The exam is written as a test of knowledge to be compared with others competing for advancement in the same rating. The tests are not written as a "qualifying" or "performance" exam. Your qualifications and performance are considered by your command prior to your recommendation for advancement.

HOW CURRENT IS THE EXAM?

The examinations are written one year in advance of the testing date. This is to ensure enough time for proofreading, printing, and distribution prior to each exam cycle. Even though the items on your exam are one year old, you must remember to answer all questions *as if the exam was printed and distributed today*. Answer all questions in accordance with procedures and publications that are effective on exam day. Anything on the exam that is not effective or outdated on exam day will not count against you.

BIBLIOGRAPHY
Just before the beginning of each year, the exam writer has to decide which publications and other reference material he wants to use for the upcoming year's examinations. Of course, the Rate Training Manuals for his rating will be on the top of this list. Any additional publications that he desires to use in research for "finding" items to place on exams must be printed on this list. This listing is known as the Bibliography for Advancement Examination Study. The "Bib" must also be broken down into applicable pay grade levels, i.e., which publications pertain to which pay grades. The important thing to remember about the "Bib" is that it is prepared by the writer before any exams are written. It is used as a list for reference purposes by the writer, and can be considered as an outline for study purposes by the examinee. The bibliography is discussed more in detail in a later chapter.

TYPES OF QUESTIONS
There are four types of questions that a writer uses on examinations. Each type is different according to the reference used.

Type "A"
The first type (we'll call it Type "A") is questions that are taken from information in the Rate Training Manual for the rating involved (Example: YN3&2, BM3&2, etc.). These are the "easy" items for the writer to "find," and probably the easiest ones for the candidates on exam day.

Type "B"
Type "B" questions are those derived from information in other publications and references listed in the Bibliography for that

year. These items are almost equally as easy to locate for the writer, but, as you can imagine, may be more difficult to answer because of the amount of material required to review. (There are only a couple or a few Rate Training Manuals for the ratings, but there may be twenty other references listed for your rating in the bibliography.)

Type "C"
Type "C" items are questions taken from publications or instructions that are referenced in the Rate Training Manual, but do not appear on the remaining list in the bibliography. (Example: You're studying for YN3. Page 49 of your YN3&2 Rate Training Manual states, "Consult OPNAVINST 4790.4 for more information concerning..."). This statement, using OPNAVINST 4790.4 as a "reference," tells the exam writer that he may go to that reference to extract information for an exam. These statements, using references in Rate Training Manuals, should be the "clue" for the advancement candidate to seek out that reference to ensure "absolute" readiness for the exam.

Type "D"
Type "D" questions are taken from publications and instructions referenced in other listings from the bibliography. (Example: NTP-3 is a publication listed in the bibliography for study at the IT3 level. If page 70 of NTP-3 stated "SECNAVINST 2300.4

provides basic Department of Defense policy for..."), that statement would leave SECNAVINST 2300.4 available to the exam writer to construct exam items from.

In order to keep the examinations realistic, the writer will construct the predominant number of items from Type "A" and "B" references. In order to keep the examinations competitive, items from Type "C" and "D" will be selected.

By now, you should be realizing why no one "aces" the exams.

ITEM WRITING

Let's discuss how the writer actually puts the exam questions together. As can be imagined, most of his time is spent in research. By reading through all the "listings" in the bibliography, he selects material to become test items. Most of the writers use a "card" system. As he arrives at a new item in a publication that is pertinent for an exam, he constructs a question about the material. He places the question on a 5" X 8" card that contains several "blocks" for information about the question. This card system may be manually kept, or maintained in a computer data base.

In one corner of the card is a space for the writer to insert the occupational standard number that pertains to the test question. These are five-digit numbers found in front of every occupational standard as listed in the Manual of Navy Enlisted Manpower and Personnel Classification and Occupational Standards (NAVPERS 18068).

Another space on the card is reserved for the appropriate pay grade for which the item is being written (i.e., "BM3," "PN2"). The card also contains a block called "bibliography." Here the writer must place the exact reference (publication, article, page number, paragraph, etc.) where he found the information.

In the center of the card, the writer types the question plus the four "choices" as they would appear on the exam. An asterisk (*) is placed next to the correct answer.

As each exam writing cycle occurs, the writer is required to write a percentage of "new" cards for each rating exam. The normal time frame for constructing an exam is 30 days.

"THE BOX"

The writer maintains a box of cards for each pay grade in his rating. These boxes contain the cards from previous examinations. The cards are the same ones that may have been prepared during last year's writing cycle, or possible those from 5 or 6 exams earlier. All of them are separated by "occupational standard" number. Once again, this "box" may be maintained as a computer data base, but you can understand the idea. The questions are "stored" for future use.

If these cards had been used on previous exams, they will have a "sticker" pasted on them reflecting the statistics of that particular question for each exam on which it has appeared. The statistics tell the writer and the education specialist how "easy" or how "difficult" the question was during its previous exam appearances. They show what percentage of the candidates selected each "choice" for each question. If a question is exhibited as too easy or too difficult, it cannot be used again until it has had considerable changes made to it.

Did anyone ever tell you that there must be "repeat" questions on exams? Maybe you have noticed this yourself. That is the purpose of the "box." The writer only has to construct a percentage (a flexible figure) of "new" items for each exam. He may go to the box to draw items for re-use, as long as the questions have good statistics.

PUTTING IT TOGETHER

The writer assembles all 200 cards with the pertinent data transcribed, including all drawings, schematics, and pictures that he wants to place on the exam. The package is then turned over to the education specialist, who checks each item for grammatical accuracy and proper style of writing. He proceeds through the exam items with a checklist to ensure such things as proper schematics appearing with the correct question, and that there is a proper distribution of correct answers keyed. (For instance, an exam cannot have 120 out of the 200 questions with "choice a" as the correct answer. There has to be a more even distribution.)

Another important thing the education specialist checks is to ensure that all occupational standards for the specific pay grade has been covered on the test. He checks to ensure that at least one question appears on the test to cover the standards listed for that rate.

After the education specialist completes his check, the exam items go to the graphics section for the preparation and placement of all pictures or schematics needed on the exam. From there it goes back to the writer for a final check before printing. After printing and final proofreading, the exam goes into stock, ready for Navy-wide distribution prior to exam day.

Writer "Updates"
How do the exam writers stay current on what is going on out in the fleet? This is done in various ways. As previously stated, they are constantly doing research in the publications, manuals, and various references pertaining to the rating. They also maintain close liaison with all schools ("A" School, "C" Schools, etc.) to obtain updated information, and ideas on future procedures.

Another most beneficial way for the writer to remain abreast of what is happening in the fleet is to actually go there. They occasionally make trips to a city/port where a large number of their rating is stationed, visit ships, and hold discussions with both junior and senior personnel in their rating.

Writer Takes Exam

There was mention earlier of a situation where there could be "outdated" material on the exam because it is written one year in advance. This is how it is updated. On the same morning the fleet takes the exam, the writer is "tested" as well. He receives a copy of the exam and goes through it item by item, physically looking up each reference to ensure that it is truly a good current specimen of testable material. If something has caused the material to be outdated, such as a change in procedures since the item was written, the item will be deleted from the exam. At that point, the exam is graded on a scale of 199 items instead of 200. This happens often, so don't get excited if you notice outdated material on exam day. Your exam gets "updated" the same time that you take it.

CHAPTER THREE

PREPARATION FOR THE EXAM

Now that you have some background on advancement and examination development, we can get into the actual preparation steps prior to the exam. Some are things that you could do **every day** on a long-term basis; others are steps to prepare for **one specific exam**. Proper preparation will instill the required confidence you need when going in to take any exam. The following tips are **sure-win** methods to assist anyone toward advancement in the Navy.

CORRESPONDENCE COURSE

Complete the correspondence course for your desired rate. Even if you are not required to complete the course due to graduation from "A" School, do it anyway. Think back to the section explaining the types of questions in this guide. The rate training manual is a **primary** reference. By completing the correspondence course, you will be providing yourself with primary information needed on test day. The questions in the correspondence course cannot be used word-for-word on the exam, but the **information** is the same. When a correspondence course is written, it must cover the occupational standards for the pay grades designated in the front of the rate training manual. These are the **same** occupational standards covered on your exam.

By completing the course, you can't miss in obtaining the required **basic** information to enable you to answer many items on the test.

RATE TRAINING MANUAL

Get your own personal copy of the rate training manual for your desired pay grade, and maintain it as a "mark up" copy. After completing the course, go through the "blue book" as if you were writing a test on the book alone. Get yourself a yellow "highlighter" pencil and shade through the major subjects that appear to be "testable" material. Think back to the list of occupational standards while you are doing this. You will recognize that many **highlighted** sections in your rate training manual equate directly to specific statements in the occupational standards listing. Each occupational standard is not usually covered only in one chapter or section of the manual. They may be spread out over a large portion of the book.

Remember to look up the **referenced material** in the rate training manual. If the manual tells you that "*more information on this subject is available in ...,*" then find that reference and keep that information with your rate training manual. This will help you in answering those "Type C" questions, and could be a determining factor in your advancement.

Pay particular attention to "figures" or graphs presented in the Rate Training Manual. These are always easy **"targets"** from which writers can develop test items.

BE A GOOD LISTENER
The best students are good listeners. They are inquisitive individuals that **"want to know"** the subject matter. They are not afraid to ask questions about new procedures, and do not "pass" on the opportunity to join in on work-related discussions.

Every office and shop in the Navy is an example of a gold mine of information. Daily discussions of procedures, methods, and doctrine in a work environment are super learning tools for good listeners. Remember, your exam writer has already worked in one of those shops/offices, and a lot of his ideas for test items will come from past experience.

Think of how many "discussions" or "arguments" occur each day in your work space where someone has to run to the shelf and "look something up" to prove the correct method of performing a task. In most cases, the individuals involved in this situation don't even realize it, but they are learning through these discussions, and the information that is "looked up" is passed on to all who listen intently. Either get in on these discussions, or be aware of them when they occur. Find out what the correct answer is.

If you spend eight hours of a day in the working presence of peers and senior personnel, and don't learn at least one **new** item of information about your rating, you have **wasted** that day by **not listening**.

FIND A GOOD "COACH"
What better way to learn anything than through the experience of others? Everyone that wants to make rate in the Navy will find that a "coach" is most helpful. Look around your work space, and pick out a senior, knowledgeable individual in your same rating. It may be your immediate supervisor, your chief, or a friend that you go on liberty with. Explain to them your desires to advance, and ask their assistance. Tell them you will be asking lots of questions.

People who have progressed in any rating take pride in the knowledge they have obtained in the process. You should make arrangements to **use** this knowledge to your advantage. Let their knowledge rub off on you, either in the form of questions and answers or work-related discussions. Any "old salt" will usually enjoy exhibiting his/her experience and wisdom through discussions with you. This means of learning is normally done in a more relaxed atmosphere, and you will be surprised how much of it you retain.

Even if you have to put up with an occasional "sea story" in the process, use a coach and his/her experience whenever possible.

GAMES

Have you ever played a "knowledge" game such as Trivial Pursuit? People that do play games such as these have found that they enjoyed a good time while learning (or reinforcing) information that they either (1) had forgotten, or (2) never knew. The material learned during these games is more permanently implanted in the mind because the process occurred under "favorable" or "fun" circumstances.

Here is an excellent means of spending those "dead" hours at work, when the time seems to drag along. Start your own "Rating Game," or "Stump the Expert" competition among your co-workers! Everyone look up an item in a publication that is related to your rating. The questions must come from a reference in the Bibliography for your rating, or from a publication that is **referenced** in a publication in the bibliography (remember the Type "C" and "D" questions). The person answering the item correctly gets to "test" the others with his researched question. If there is an argument over a response provided, the person presenting the question must be prepared to provide the correct reference to the group.

Another "game" that can provide active preparation for exams is "Question of the Day." Post a chalk board in your work area in a conspicuous place. Each day, an appointed person places a question taken from a Bibliography reference on the chalk board. Anyone in the group may place the answer on the board, and discussion of the item will inevitably follow.

By using "games" such as these at work, you are performing one of the same functions that the exam writer does in the preparation of the exam - **the RESEARCH**. You will be pleasantly surprised to realize how much information is learned and retained in your memory from these "games."

Remember the theory: If you leave an 8-hour day without learning at least **ONE new item** about your occupational field, then you have **WASTED** that day!

TRAINING PLANS

Volunteer as an instructor in your division/department training program. Ask your training petty officer to include you as an active participant in the work center training. Get some example training plans from him, and develop your own plan **from scratch** on each subject that you will be teaching.

Along with being an excellent administrative training tool for your more senior years, the development of these training plans will force you to **research** and **write about** the subject matter. When you actually speak about the subject to a group, you are less likely to forget the material.

This works! Ask around your command and take notice of how many senior chiefs and master chiefs have had formal Instructor School training. They have had the experience of training plan development, and they know how to perform the **research function.**

THE NOTEBOOK

This is where a lot of people "miss the boat." Every candidate for advancement should develop a "binder" notebook for his/her study and constant review. The notebook should be started early in a career and kept current by constant updates, corrections, and additions whenever required. This notebook can be your **personal guide** to advancement. Notes from classroom training, formal schools, and any material you find interesting in research can be included in this notebook.

CAUTION: If you keep CLASSIFIED notes in your notebook, they must be kept in a secure space, and you CANNOT take them home. When you transfer, your classified notes can be mailed (through your security officer) to your next command.

A weekly or monthly update of your notebook should be sufficient. Material within the notebook should be categorized by major subject area, and should pertain to your next prospective pay grade plus all lower pay grades within your rating. Save all the material you have inserted in your notebook for previous pay grades. You will see a lot of this material on **future exams**.

"ABSOLUTE" PREPARATIONS
Listed below are a few "must" items you should use and procedures to follow in preparing for any Navy-wide advancement examination.

  (1) **Occupational Standards** - Review the list of occupational standards for your desired pay grade before you begin your program of study. These "OCC STDS" are the **minimum requirements** for your rate as set forth by the Chief of Naval Personnel. This list will inform a candidate of what performances are expected of him/her in the specific pay grade

on the test. Remember: The writer must cover all the Occupational Standards for the specified pay grade on the test; so, by reviewing this list, you will learn the **basic** testing criteria.

(2) **Bibliography** - This is a "must use" item. You cannot properly prepare for the test without use of the bibliography. The listed bibliography provides the **source material** used by the writer to support the questions on exams. This "bib" is **updated annually**, so make sure you are working with a copy of the current edition. The year printed on the front of the bibliography sheet should be the same year you are taking the exam. The Naval Education and Training Program Management Support Activity in Pensacola, Florida produces a booklet for each Navy rating called "(year) Occupational Standards and Bibliography." They are usually about 15 pages long (printed in booklet form), and are distributed Navy-wide for the exam candidates' use. Your command career counselor or training officer should receive these in the mail in plenty of time before the beginning of each calendar year. Obtain your own personal copy of this booklet each year. If it isn't onboard your command, ask your career counselor to order them. The use of these bibliographies is a necessary tool in studying. Their importance cannot be stressed strongly enough. **USE THE BIBLIOGRAPHY**.

(3) **Exam Subject Matter ID Sheets** - If you are taking a specific exam for the first time, find someone who has previously taken the same test. Ask to see the Subject-Matter Identification Sheet that was presented the person on exam day. Reviewing this sheet from a previous exam will show you the major areas covered by the writer. These areas can change from test to test, but in most cases, they remain very similar. This does not give you an automatic "heads up" on what to expect on a forthcoming exam, but it will provide a general idea of what is covered on an exam in your rate.

(4) **Study Schedule** - Plan a study schedule. Try to set up study time for the same time and same place each day. Study when you are alert. Take breaks to prevent one long period of study. Pick a comfortable place to study with minimum distractions. Set up short-term study goals, and reward yourself when you reach them. For instance, promise yourself a rest break after mastering two or three chapters. Your schedule should be made up well in advance of the test. "Cramming" usually won't work here due to the scope of material to be

studied. You may have to remind yourself of the reason **why you are studying**. Remember your motivation factor here. Reminding yourself of the possible benefits will establish your **will to learn**, and therefore improve your concentration level during study.

(5) **Review Junior Material** - If you are studying for E-5 or above, ALWAYS review the material from the lower pay grades in your rating. This is where the notebook idea will come in handy. Remember "the box" the writer has for each pay grade. You are held responsible for this "junior" material, and the exam writer will use it as a good "target area" for test items. Many chief petty officer candidates leave exams saying they noticed a lot of questions from their 3rd class petty officer days. Don't just study the items marked in the Bibliography for your *desired* pay grade. Review everything *below* it as well.

(6) **Pre-Test Checks** - Everyone must fill out or sign a "worksheet" prior to the exam. The command Education Services Officer usually fills out the worksheet and the candidate simply signs it. **Check the worksheet carefully**. Ensure your time-in-grade and time-in-service is annotated correctly. One area you may want to pay particular attention to is the AWARDS block. If you have a Good Conduct Medal or certain other awards (such as a Letter of Commendation from a Flag Officer) you will be granted "points" on the exam for these awards. Ensure you get the proper credit when reviewing your examination worksheet.

If you are an E-7 candidate, it is imperative that you send for a copy of your Enlisted Summary Record. This is to ensure that the selection board is seeing everything that they should see when your Enlisted Summary Record comes up for review. To obtain a copy of your ESR, write to:

Navy Personnel Command, Pers 312
5720 Integrity Drive
Millington TN 38055-3120

Your request must contain your full name, social security number, rate, return address, and signature. You may want to check with your personnel office for a possible update on the above address. Requests take several weeks, so mail early.
Bupers also has a secure login site where you may view your ESR.

CRAMMING AS A LAST RESORT

The correct way to prepare for any Navy-wide examination is to **properly review** if you have time, and "cram" only if you don't. Test-makers and educators have made the word "cram" a dirty word. They have naturally tried to discourage any system that a candidate may use as a substitute from "normal" studying. They do this because cramming is *not the best way* to learn and retain information.

Cramming is a perfectly respectable technique for occasions when time is unavoidably short. It is an approach similar to what a newspaper reporter uses in order to make his deadline. Cramming is best used to **supplement** a reasonable period of **normal** study.

If you absolutely have to cram, review as actively as possible. Use pencil and paper, outlining the material and underlining the portions of pages that you feel are good test items. At this point, treat your "review" like a contest between you and the test writer. Scan only the **major references** listed in the Bibliography while trying to "out-think" the exam writer.

EXAM DAY

Now is the time when you can cash in on all your efforts. But, all your careful preparation could be wasted if you are not careful.

When you are given your exam, review the front cover of the examination sheet along with the proctor, and follow directions explicitly. Your correct social security number and name spelling are most important. An error in your social security number, such as filling in the circle for a "3" instead of a "2," will cause the computer in Pensacola to reject your exam due to "Unmatched SSN." This could delay your exam results as much as two months.

Read through the entire exam thoroughly before you start making marks on the answer sheet. By noticing some of the questions in advance, your subconscious mind will be provided time to form some of the answers. Remain calm and relaxed while doing this. Remember, you must not attain the attitude of "fighting" the test.

Every Question Must Have A Response
Go through your answer sheet after you have completed the test to insure that there are no unmarked items. Go down each row on the exam answer sheet, making sure that there is a response filled in for each question. If you find an unanswered question, locate it in the test booklet to determine what you did wrong. After answering the question, go back and forward at least five questions each way in your test booklet to verify that they are also answered correctly. There is always the possibility of an earlier or later error on the test, causing that one specific question to be left unanswered.

Mismarks
As a final verification, go through your items one by one to assure yourself that you have actually filled in the correct circle for each question. Remember that this is only a check of your hand-eye coordination. This is not the time to start changing answers. It is only a check to verify that you responded the way you intended to. Start at question #1, reading each stem and identifying the answer you have selected. Refer to the answer

sheet to determine if that is the response that you actually marked.

YOUR REVIEW AFTER THE TEST
The time you spend immediately after the exam is crucial to future exams you will be taking in your rating throughout your career. You will see the same subject areas and many of the same items again on future exams, no matter what pay grade is tested. You can bet your chevrons on it!

This is one of the reasons why you should **NEVER** leave an exam early. Use all the allotted time in reviewing your exam, and remember as much about it as you can.

Major Areas
After you depart the examination room, go directly to a quiet, secluded spot and start making notes. Draw from your memory such things as the major areas covered on the exam. Make an outline on paper of these major areas.

Make an attempt to remember all the questions in each area, with particular emphasis placed on the most difficult items. If more than one person took the same examination, you may want to pool your resources in this effort.

Construct your list of questions in a rough format as soon as possible, while the information is still fresh in your mind.

Looking Up The "Unknowns"
Mark the questions that you did not know the answer to, and look them up while the exact wording of the item is still in your memory. Put an asterisk (*) next to those items to "flag" your memory in the future that this was a gray area on a previous exam.

Add To Your Notebook
Put all the items that you can remember from the test into your notebook of study material. You are now adding to your "book" of knowledge in your rating. This can serve as a review "tool" prior to your next exam.

Flash Cards

If you are especially energetic, and want to invest some time to benefit all your future examination scores, put all the items you can remember on flash cards. You can easily obtain packages of 3"X5" cards, and place a question on the front side and an answer on the back side of each card. Add to these as you see fit, cataloging them by major area as they would appear in exams. Review them at your convenience in your spare time. This "spare time" will soon be known as "quality time" spent toward your future.

Tape Recorder

As stated before, hearing things and discussion tends to implant information into our memory with more permanence than reading. If you place your items of information on tape, you will have a ready reference to listen to in any of your leisure time. If you have a tape player in your car, the opportune time to listen to your test items on tape is each day while driving to and from work. This is a great way to pass the time during traffic jams.

Use Your Profile And Exam Info Sheets

After the results of your exam are published, you will receive an Examination Profile Sheet, informing you of your performance on each area of the test. These profile sheets provide you with another excellent opportunity for review. It will tell you which major areas you must spend more time on in order to improve your future test scores. Use these profile sheets for review, even if you have advanced on that particular exam. This is when you should start investing time toward your next exam, even if it is for the next pay grade two years down the road. Remember, knowledge and proper preparation are the foundations of advancement.

CHAPTER FOUR

FUNDAMENTAL "RULES" TO REMEMBER

This section deals with basic phrases associated with the construction of exams, and some important "laws" to live by when attacking the test on exam day. By familiarizing yourself with this section, you will be better prepared to handle any type question that may appear on an exam.

TEST PHRASES
Each test item (question) is composed of two parts, the stem and the alternatives. The stem is the beginning statement, or question, that provides the problem for you to answer. The alternatives of the question are the four choices (on all Navy-wide exams) that you select from to answer the question correctly. Other words for alternatives are "responses," "options," or "choices." The alternatives are labeled A, B, C, and D. These four alternatives are broken down into a "correct" choice, plus three "distracters," or incorrect answers. The purpose of this guide is to help you to select the correct alternatives from the distracters.

METHODS BY WHICH YOU MAY ANSWER
Almost every test item will have to be approached in a different manner. This approach also depends on how well you prepared yourself for the exam. Here are some different methods you may have to use in answering test questions:

1. **Absolute Recall** - This is the very best way to answer an item, because you absolutely know the answer, probably without looking at the alternatives offered. These are the kind of items we all look forward to on an exam - the confidence builders - the ones that set you at ease and give you a good feeling toward the rest of the test.

2. **Process of Elimination** - This is sometimes called "deduction." It is one of the primary approaches you should take on test items. At times you can eliminate some (or all but one) of the distracters by the process of elimination, leaving you with the

correct answer, or at least fewer distracters to pick from. This is an important skill to learn, and it will help you get through some of the more difficult questions.

3. **Association** - This is helpful on only some multiple-choice questions. You can determine the correct answer by associating the elements of these type items.

4. **Math** - Many exams require a lot of "computing" the correct answer. Technical ratings usually have these type items in areas such as electronics, electricity, navigation tables, time zones, etc.

5. **Clues in the Test Construction** - Every test has these type clues. You must know what to look for in determining these clues. The "Thinking With Exam Writer Strategy" section of this guide has more in-depth information on what to look for.

6. **"Educated" Guess** - This is when you have a strong feeling, or "hunch" that a particular answer is correct. This is where the candidate can pick up points on the exam from his "partial" knowledge of the subject, along with the areas that he absolutely knows. Don't just give up when you arrive at a difficult question and pick a "random" answer.

7. **"Unqualified" Guess** - This is what the candidate should use when all else fails, when there is absolutely no recall. On any Navy-wide exam, if you are left with the choice between leaving the question blank, and guessing, always guess. Never leave an item blank on the answer sheet. You are graded on the number of correct answers only.

LAWS

Consider these guidelines to assist you toward a successful test. One of the first things to remember is to avoid panic when approaching test time. It doesn't hurt to have a little adrenaline flowing to achieve a more alert state, but worrying about the exam will definitely be to your disadvantage. Proper preparation, as discussed in this guide, can help to avoid the worry and strain an exam can place on your mind.

Trick Questions

Do not try to read something into a test question that really isn't there. Take each word at its face value. The wording of each stem has been very carefully chosen by the writer, and checked by an education specialist. Nothing is there in an attempt to trick you.

"We Don't Do It That Way Here"

Base your correct answers on the material you have read and studied, and not on your local operating procedures. In most cases, Standard Operating Procedures (SOPs) are written using proper references, but are "tailored" to meet the needs of the local command. Always go with what is in "the book," and not by "the way we do it at my command." Remember, the exam writer does not have copies of your SOPs. He only uses the official Navy publications as reference material.

Outdated Material

Do not panic on outdated questions. Remember that the exam is written one year prior to exam day, and you should answer with the current correct answer. If the correct answer does not appear as one of the alternative, then pick the most correct answer, or even the prior correct answer. Rest assured that the question will be thrown out on exam day by the writer when he discovers it is outdated.

Stay Interested
Use common sense while reading the stem of each item, and try to decide what the writer is looking for in a correct answer. Try to control your attitude toward the "I don't like this type" questions. Force yourself to stay interested in each item, no matter how difficult it may be.

Be Careful
Select your responses and very carefully mark them on your answer sheet. Periodically check the exam item against the answer sheet to ensure that you have not missed an item, or fallen behind on the answer sheet. One out-of-sequence mark can cause all the items following it to be scored wrong. When and if you erase, do a neat, complete job of it. Don't make careless errors.

Here are some helpful guidelines to remember:

Easy Questions First

Don't waste time by pondering over the very difficult items. By doing so, you will bring on the discouraging attitude you must refrain from obtaining.

Try going through each exam in the following manner:

Slowly and carefully read the stem of each question, while picking out the key phrases and words. Attempt to answer the question without looking at the four alternatives. Then, take a look at the alternatives to see if your choice is among them. If you find it, mark your choice and move on to the next question. If your choice is not among the alternatives, read the complete question again, this time eliminating as many distracters as you can, and record the remaining possible answers on your scratch paper. (Just make a note of the question number and the remaining possible answers.) Now, you must force yourself to forget all about that question and move on.

Concentrate on only one answer at a time. Remember the steps. If, after reading the question twice, you cannot determine the correct answer, eliminate as many distracters as you can, record the choices remaining on your scratch paper, and start on the next question. This will help to save you precious minutes of time during the exam. You will have ample time remaining after going through the exam completely to return and tackle these "difficult" items. This method will also save you the discouragement of "sweating" for long periods of time over one item. You must do everything to retain that positive attitude.

Hard Questions Become Easier

As you have gone through and answered the easy questions, you have brought your mental concentration powers to a peak. Now is the time to return to the first of the "difficult" questions, and read it again. If you have previously marked down some possible options for correct answers on your scratch paper, only consider these alternatives in choosing the correct answer.

At this point you will arrive at an amazing discovery. You will see that suddenly these "difficult" questions seem to get easier! As you progressed through the test on the easy questions, you steadily increased your level of concentration, and your mind had become more permanently "fixed" on the subject at hand. At this point, you are more able to handle the more difficult items that you had problems with earlier. New thoughts have surfaced concerning the subject matter, plus you have had the advantage of being exposed to many items that may have provided "hints" toward correctly answering other questions. Often, the insight provided by the easy questions will "turn on" a chain of thought leading to the correct answer of more difficult items.

Time

You are normally allowed 3 hours (180 minutes) to complete the 200 question Navy-wide advancement exam. Simple division tells us that you have54 seconds for each question. With this information readily available, you can pace yourself accordingly. By answering the easy items first, you will not need anywhere close to the allotted time in order to answer them. You will always have a considerable amount of time to devote to the more difficult questions. By using the method of jotting down the difficult item numbers and remaining possible alternatives, you have saved even more time.

A person unskilled in this technique would have to go back and review each difficult item completely, by reading the stem and all four alternatives. If you have already eliminated some of the alternatives, you now have less material to work with. Here's an example:

You found question number 38 to be difficult, so you write the number 38 on your scratch paper. You were also able to eliminate two of the alternatives (say they were "B" and "D"). After you have answered all the easier questions, you return to your more difficult ones listed on your scratch paper. Now question number 38 only has two alternatives ("A" and "C") to pick from, neatly annotated on your scratch paper. By initially eliminating one or two distracters whenever possible, you spend less time reconsidering the remaining options.

Write down your start time, mid-point time, and scheduled finish time on the top of your scratch paper. Record your start time, and compute an hour and a half forward for your mid-point time. This mid-point time should be used to check your progress at the half-way point. You should be at least on question 75 at this point on any Navy-wide exam. This goal could be flexible, according to how many "difficult" items you may have recorded on your scratch paper. If you are behind at mid-point, you will know that you must "pick up the pace." Always work as rapidly as possible, but carefully, without sacrificing accuracy. Once you think about it, one minute and twelve seconds is a long time allowed per question. Try counting to 72 and notice how long it really is. The average easy question should take no more than 15-20 seconds each, leaving plenty of time for the difficult items, plus the "final checks."

When You Want To Change Your Answer

You have selected an alternative, and while going over your exam, you want to change you response. Many advisors discourage changing answers, feeling that your first response was probably the closest to being correct. Here is a theory to live by when you have the desire to change an answer:

Only change your first response if you have absolute, positive evidence that the first response is wrong. You must have undeniable proof of your decision.

Here are some conditions that would provide a reason to change an answer that you have already marked:

(1) You originally misread the question.

(2) The correct answer was revealed somewhere else in the test.

(3) You "skimmed over" a pertinent fact about the item, and "caught" it later, or

(4) You recall information which had not occurred to you the first time you read the question.

NEVER change an answer on a hunch! Your first impression is usually correct.

Guess Work

When does a person guess? When all other techniques fail, and you do not know the answer, by all means guess. Always! You are not penalized for guessing on Navy-wide exams. You are only graded on the number of CORRECT answers, so why not take the chance and mark something for each item? On the multiple choice exam with four alternatives, you still have a 25% chance of hitting the correct choice. There should never be an excuse for not marking something down for each question. The average person answers one out of every four guesses correctly. Add to this the test-taking skills you will learn from this guide, and you will surely answer more than 1/4 of the "guess" questions correctly. Remember the discussion on eliminating alternatives for difficult items. If you could eliminate just ONE alternative (distracter) from the item, and then guess, you have increased the percentages of a correct answer on a guess to 33% from 25%. Try it on your next exam. It works!

Your percentage can also be raised by the simple fact that you may have worked with or studied the material a long time ago, and do not recall specific details. On these occasions, even if you think you're guessing your subconscious mind will automatically make the correct choice.

CHAPTER FIVE

THINKING WITH EXAM WRITER STRATEGY

While moving from item to item through any Navy-wide examination, the candidate must develop the skill of "thinking like the exam writer." This is not a matter of "outguessing" or "outsmarting" the writer, but just keeping up with him. A human develops the questions, and in many cases, a little human instinct and training can assist in answering the items correctly. After studying this chapter, you may want to test yourself in how you are gaining through the use of this guide. Take a correspondence course, and look through some of the questions without looking up the answers in the text. You should be able to make several correct choices, even **without any previous knowledge** of the subject matter.

THE LONGEST ANSWER

The correct answer is normally the main concern of the test writer. Therefore, he/she will often spend more time (and words) with the correct response. Distracters (untrue alternatives) can be stated in just a few words. Sufficient time is not normally spent developing good distracters because of the concern given to the correct answer. The writer usually spends more time **QUALIFYING** or **JUSTIFYING** the correct answer to ensure it is absolutely true. In many instances, this process requires more words than the incorrect responses. **OVERALL RESULTS**: The correct response is usually longer in length than the three incorrect alternatives. This fact is especially helpful if the candidate is not sure of the correct answer. Whenever you are uncertain, go with the longest alternative.

EXAMPLE
What is the advantage of the use of the 1MC circuit by the commanding officer as a means of communications with the crew?

    A. It ensures an attentive audience
    B. It establishes two-way communication
    C. It allows feedback
    D. It is an excellent means of allowing the commanding officer to speak without interruption

EXAMPLE

The family services program is available to assist which of the following?

    A. Dependents only
    B. Enlisted personnel only
    C. All active and retired members of the United States Navy and their dependents
    D. Active duty personnel only

THE NEGATIVE QUESTION

First, let me give you an example of a negative question:

Which of the following ranks are NOT used in the United States Navy?

    A. Commander
    B. Lieutenant General
    C. Lieutenant Commander
    D. Captain

Negative questions often confuse the person taking the test. Under normal circumstances, the negative word is capitalized or typed in italics to "stand out" from the rest of the stem. When you notice this type of question, try reversing the question by deleting the negative word; therefore making a POSITIVE statement. Using this manner, the candidate will be answering "No" to the correct response. This should help to clear up confusion that may occur along with the anxiety of exam day. Here's another example:

EXAMPLE

All of the following are types of United States Naval ships EXCEPT

    A. Frigate
    B. Destroyer
    C. Corvette
    D. Aircraft Carrier

If you delete the word EXCEPT in the stem, you will have to answer "No" to choice "C." This method should help you in easily arriving at the correct response with minimum confusion when attacking negative questions.

CHOICES THAT OVERLAP EACH OTHER
This type of question often appears in statistical or mathematics sections of exams.

EXAMPLE
What percentage of persons treated at Navy alcoholism treatment centers are able to resume their careers after treatment?

    A. less than 60%
    B. less than 70%
    C. more than 70%
    D. more than 80%

Look at choices (A) and (B) first. It is apparent that "less than 60%" is included in "less than 70%," so you can "scratch" choice (A) as a possibility in order to avoid two correct answers. Choice (C) also overlaps into choice (D), whereas "more than 70%" can also be included in "more than 80%." (If choice (D) is correct, then choice (C) also has to be correct. By watching for this type of question, you can easily cut down a four-alternative question to be a less complicated two-choice item. In the above example, since (A) encompasses (B), and choice (C) overlaps into (D), the correct choice would have to be between alternatives (B) and (C).

ALTERNATIVES THAT ARE SIMILAR
Some test items that you encounter will have options that are very closely related and almost identical.

EXAMPLE
Unless further action is taken, naval message directives are automatically canceled after what period of time following the date of release?

    A. 1 year
    B. 6 months
    C. 90 days
    D. 180 days

Just by "catching" or identifying this type question, you have considerably narrowed your choices. The similar choices (B) and (D) **cannot BOTH** be correct, and you must select the **MOST CORRECT** answer. If two choices are closely related or similar in completeness and scope, the **CORRECT** answer is usually an alternative **OTHER THAN the related ones**.

You may think that the example provided is an exaggerated one because of alternatives (B) and (D) meaning relatively the same thing, but this situation often occurs when the writer is searching for distracters (wrong answers) to place in an item after the correct alternative has been identified. Watch for them closely.

POSITION OF THE CORRECT ANSWER

The position of an alternative can sometimes identify its degree of correctness. In almost all cases, the alternatives will be placed in ascending or descending order. Take a look at the following example.

EXAMPLE

According to Navy industrial safety records, what number of minor injuries occur for each severe injury?

    A. 15 to 20
    B. 20 to 25
    C. 25 to 30
    D. 30 to 35

The numbers either go from low to high, or from high to low. Test construction methods recommend **enclosing** the correct answer between alternatives of higher or lower value. This is normally a clue that the correct answer is **not** the highest or lowest value, but one in between. Therefore, if you absolutely **do not know** the answer, a good choice would be to give primary consideration to the middle two (B or C) options. Of course, if you are **sure** of the answer after reading the stem, don't even consider this strategy. In the above example, (C) is the correct choice.

Another thing to consider in this strategy is the fact that it is normal for the test writer to "bury" the correct alternative between two extreme alternatives on complex questions. The writer may shy away from keying (A) as the correct answer, because when a candidate does not know the answer, he will be tempted to mark (A), and move on. So, the writer would prefer that the candidates "hunt" for the correct answer.

REMEMBER: This strategy is only for use when you are completely stumped for a correct answer, and should only be used in that situation. After all, the correct responses to all items on a test cannot be (B) or (C). Navy exam writers are told how they must **evenly distribute** the correctly keyed alternatives on each exam, so if you notice that all (or most) of your choices are ending up keyed as (B) or (C), then you should realize the error of your ways.

"ALL OF THE ABOVE"

Most people treat these type questions with more difficulty than they deserve. To decide whether or not the "all of the above" alternative is the correct one, all you have to do is treat it like a TRUE or FALSE question. Either "all of the above" is true, or it is not. If you feel that the "all of the above" choice may be the correct one, try to identify two of the alternatives that **are** correct responses. (Two is all you need.) If you can find two, then the correct response **has to be** "all of the above." No sense in wasting time on the other response that is left over. If two of them are correct, the answer is automatically "all of the above."

Thinking in the reverse mode now; if you can identify **one** alternative that is **not correct**, then the answer cannot be that alternative, **NOR** "all of the above," so you will be left with only two other choices from which to choose. All you have to do is find one "distracter," and you have increased your chances of a correct response from **25% to 50%**.

Take a look at the following examples, and you will see how this system works.

EXAMPLE

Material readiness aboard U. S. Navy surface ships includes which of the following conditions?

    A. YOKE
    B. XRAY
    C. ZEBRA
    D. All of the above

Assume that the candidate knows alternatives (A) and (B) to be correct. If that is the case, then the answer absolutely has to be (D). In this type question, if two choices are correct, then they are all correct.

EXAMPLE

Which of the following is/are important reason(s) why sound-powered telephones should always be unplugged when not in use?

        A. To conserve the batteries
        B. To prevent the circuit from short circuiting
        C. To prevent unwanted sound from entering the circuit.
        D. All of the above

Now, I'm going to go ahead and assume that we all know that there are no batteries in sound powered circuits. So, once we can determine that alternative (a) is **not** correct, we can automatically discount alternative (D) as a possibility, leaving us with only (B) and (C) to choose from. Now we are up to a 50% possibility of a correct answer, even if we do not know that choice (C) is the correct alternative.

ANSWER DISCLOSED BY ANOTHER QUESTION

The process of constructing a Navy-wide examination is a difficult one. This difficulty leads to the remote but very real possibility that one question may inadvertently answer another question later in the exam. The exam writer may have had a most difficult time in the process of assembling 150 good items to place on the exam, much less making an attempt at cross-referencing them. Look at the following example, and you will see what to watch out for on exams:

EXAMPLE

Question # 16 may ask:

16. *The circuit designation of the Captain's Battle Circuit is*

    A. JA
    B. JL
    C. 1JV
    D. JC

Then, later in the exam, question # 89 may ask:

89. *The proper manner for the controller of the JA Captain's Battle Circuit to find out if telephone stations are manned and ready is to state*

    A. "Radio check"
    B. "All stations sound off"
    C. "All stations, control, testing"
    D. "Aye Aye"

In this example, the stem of question # 89 gave away the answer to item # 16. Even if you did not know the correct response for item # 89, it would have provided you with the correct answer to # 16, if you were paying attention.

REPEATED ALTERNATIVES

These are always fun. Suppose that, knowing very little about Navy ship types, you were faced with this item:

EXAMPLE

Two types of amphibious warfare ships are

        A. DD and LCC
        B. LCC and LPD
        C. LPD and PHM
        D. ATF and ARS

There is no perfect alternative to knowledge of the subject, but the calm application of reasoning and logic - coupled with some shrewd guessing - can be a lot better than nothing at all. Notice in the previous example that two types of ships (and only two) are mentioned more than once. The reason these are repeated is to make the item more difficult for those that can only remember one of the ships in this category. Once you find the two that are mentioned twice, you should choose the alternative that contains both of them.

Lets look at another example of a question with repeated alternatives:

EXAMPLE

What two types of measurements are taken whenever a ship has been exposed to radiation or has been radiologically contaminated?

        A. Intensity of radiation field and blood damage
        B. Total dosage received and intensity of radiation field
        C. Nitrogen mustard and cyanide
        D. Tear agent and total dosage received

Notice that "intensity of radiation" and "total dosage received" are used twice in order to disqualify those candidates who may not know both tests. By simply noting the repeated alternatives, and finding them mentioned together, you can correctly choose (B) as the answer.

CHAPTER SIX

YOUR MEMORY

Your memory is by far the most remarkable of all your mental functions. Everything you do is made easier by the use of your memory. Every activity is made simpler by the fact that you have had some previous experience that told your mind and body how to react to specific situations. The fact that you can read this guide is proof that you are using your memory. The practical application of memory use is a most important aspect of preparing for Navy-wide examinations.

"BAD" OR "GOOD" MEMORY?
No one is stuck with a "bad" memory, or even blessed with a "good" memory. Memory is a process, so when we say someone has a good memory; we are really saying that they are good at memory skills. The process of remembering can be improved just as your skill at tennis or golf can be upgraded. The reasons that cause poor memory skills can be identified, and steps can be taken to correct the problem.

CAUSES OF WHY WE FORGET THINGS
There are several reasons why we have problems in remembering items from our day-to-day activities at work or during study. Here are some "memory blocks" to look out for.

"Not Interested"

Memory storage on any one subject is directly related to the amount of interest devoted to it. The less interested you are in a particular item, the less you will remember about it. You've seen it happen or done it hundreds of times. Think about it. You meet someone on the street but don't remember his or her name ten minutes later. You probably weren't interested in meeting him/her in the first place. A used car salesman quotes a price of an automobile to you on the car lot, but you don't remember the price quoted when you arrive home. You didn't want that car from the beginning. You flunked the college algebra test because you "couldn't stay interested" in it. Your degree of interest can be a confusing factor; not only to the people around you, but also within your own mind as well. Sometimes you will think you are interested in items that you really don't care about at all. You also may be curious enough about the subject, but not be in the proper frame of mind to retain the information.

Negative Thinking
How often have you heard someone say, "I'm awful at remembering names," or "I can never remember any figures or numbers." This is a person reinforcing his own lack of recall capabilities. This is a habit that encourages the mind not to even try to remember things.

The repeating of the statement (or thinking that way) provides the excuse for failure to remember. Don't degrade the ability of your memory. Eliminate negative thoughts and **believe** that your memory will work for you.

Lack of Use

The memory must be used in order to keep functioning properly. Psychologists have found that, on the average, we forget over seventy percent of what we've learned within one hour, and over eighty percent after two days! These figures apply to the use of memory after initial learning situations.

Weak Impressions

It's very easy to forget things that never made a strong impression on you to begin with. This can be caused by not properly paying attention, not thinking the idea was important, or not taking the proper time to learn the item.

Interference

A poor learning environment during study or confusing activities afterwards can cause interference in your memory. For instance, it is not a good idea to study your rate training manual and then go immediately to a football game. It is more difficult to remember or retain things when study is followed by a period of excitement or emotional intensity. Your mind would experience too much interference for easy recall.

Repressing Information

Repressing, or squelching something from your consciousness develops as a result of mental blocks that we consciously or unconsciously set up. Many of us have repressed certain negative events from our childhood. This same ability to "muffle" or "smother" things grows with us, and we find that even useful information ends up being forgotten. So, mental blocks set up to avoid unnecessary emotional trauma could easily be used by our subconscious to squelch information that we really need.

STEPS TO A BETTER MEMORY

Now we have read about some of the causes of less-than-sharp recall ability. The ideas on the following pages will provide you with thoughts that will assist you in maintaining a fine-tuned memory.

Pay Attention
The first step is being aware of what you are studying. Begin to notice what part of each page has the "meat" of the information.

Take notice of how the material is presented, paying particular attention to any graphs or figures featured on the pages. Get the information correct in your mind the first time you read about it. Read it carefully with a purpose toward understanding the material. Focus on numbers and statistics.

Faith in Yourself
By telling yourself that you **can** remember the material, you will help to develop your own self-image. Faith in yourself relaxes and encourages stronger mental processes through opening previously closed thought process channels. You can only do what you **believe** you can accomplish.

Attitude
Your attitude has a major effect on the memorization process. You must **want** to remember what you hear, see, and read. If you view the material as a mental "block" or "barrier" to your learning, it will remain as one until you change your attitude. An optimistic view toward the subject matter will clear all the early cobwebs and doubts from your mind. The correct attitude can put you on the road to some very resourceful learning practices.

Develop Desire

In most cases, the incentive to remember the material is already there. Everyone wants to advance. But every object of memory is made stronger when you **intensify** your **desire** to be able to recall the information.

Constantly remind yourself that the material you are studying is **testable**, and your efforts will increase appreciably.

Establish a Goal

Every memory problem is easier to carry through when you let yourself know beforehand exactly what it is that you are trying to do. Outline the task in your mind, and by doing so, you will establish a pattern for your memory to complete. This will assist your mind to organize the material as a "total" subject, and will help in the areas of association and recall. By establishing a goal for your memory to work with, you have prepared a curriculum of sorts, letting your mind "gauge" your progress. This will also reinforce your ability to recall previous information about the subject.

Be Creative

Unleash your imagination. Turn your text material into pictures. Exaggerate and be artistic. Think of what equipment **looks** like when reading about it. Form a picture in your mind. Take graphs and figures from your text and associate it with how it works at your command.

Use Repetition

Refresh your memory with a review, preferably within an hour after you learn it. Most of what we learn is maintained in our "short-term" memory until we repeat it a few times. An example is a phone number that you look up in the phone directory. You can remember it long enough to dial the number once you close the book. If the phone number is busy, you probably have to look it up again if you wait ten minutes before redialing. To have data transferred to your long-term memory, you must repeat it and use it for reinforcement. Try studying in four one-hour sessions instead of one four-hour session, and spend a few minutes at the beginning of each session reviewing notes from the last sessions. This will help to place information in your long-term memory.

Mental Pictures
Your mind will store images and pictures more easily than words. Whenever possible, try to form paragraphs from your text into a mental picture. When reading about equipment, for example, visualize what the gear looks like while reading about capabilities, restrictions, etc., of the equipment.   You perform this process every day without realizing it.   If you want to remember what kind of beer you drank last night, you don't recall the letters *M-i-l-l-e-r L-i-t-e;* you only visualize the picture of the bottle or can and pick out the label. You can easily convert this process to use while studying your research material for exams.

Association
This is the simplest method of remembering. It is the process of recalling a single item because something else reminded you of it. By being aware of how one idea can relate to another, and by the use of mental pictures, you can easily recall to memory any information about any subject. The possibilities are unlimited in this area. This trait of your memory probably would work best if you construct exaggerated associations, devise funny reminders, or visualize the subject in ridiculous settings while studying them.

Reduce The Interference Factor
Try to cut down on the distractions that affect your retention of material, both during and after study periods. It is a good idea to do your studying prior to a period of rest, or at night just before you go to sleep. This will allow your mind to be in a relaxed state and will enhance the storage capacity of information.

"Recall" Exercises
Make attempts at sharpening your recall abilities. If you run across a subject that has critical information (you **know** it **has** to be included on the exam), make up flash cards on 3X5-inch index cards. Carry them with you whenever possible. Take them out and practice recalling the information while waiting for the bus, standing in line at the cafeteria, or taking a break in the lounge. You will be surprised how much this tactic helps. All this "dead" time put to use with flash cards will also inform you of

how much "wasted" time you had on your hands before you started using it effectively.

Reinforcement

When you are studying a subject, and know that you have the ability to repeat it verbatim, from start to finish (or even backwards), it is a good idea to take a short break. Then go back and re-study the entire material that you just finished. This will provide reinforcement for your memory to be able to recall the information for a longer period of time. After you have reinforced the subject in your mind, try to perform activities that do not require too much thinking (or excitement) for awhile.

If you are going to forget part of what you learned, you will forget the largest portion of it very shortly after you have learned it for the first time. You may study 50 items one day, but can only remember 25 of them the next day. If you re-study the 25 you've forgotten, by the next day you may know 40 of the original 50. If you then study the 10 you have forgotten, you will have mastered all 50 items. The important thing to remember is that the **sooner** you can review (reinforce) what you've learned, the better your memory will recall it.

Effective "Breaks"

Studying for short periods of time, with effective break periods in between used for relaxation, will usually produce a longer-lasting memory of new items than one long, drawn-out study session. Only so much information can be "crammed" into the memory at one time. If you try studying the subject matter for an hour, take a fifteen minute break, then go back to studying for an hour, another break, and so on, you should see that you have learned and retained more information. During one prolonged period of study without breaks, you will find your mind wandering into several different areas. The break periods will allow you to reason the material out into your own thoughts, and will assist the material to "sink in."

READ WITH YOUR HAND

As a child, we were all taught **not** to do this. Try it and you will see that it helps increase your speed, comprehension, and plants things more easily in your memory. It will build up speed in reading because it prevents unnecessary backing up and re-reading which consumes about one-sixth of our reading time. It also prevents prolonged staring at one word or phrase (daydreaming). Reading with your hand on the page improves your comprehension by directing to a certain spot instead of allowing your eyes and mind to wander. Try placing your fingertip under the lines while you read. **It helps!**

CHAPTER SEVEN

PROGRAMMING YOUR SUBCONSCIOUS MIND

Earlier in this guide, you found discussions concerning study habits, concentration, and memory in preparing for Navy-wide examinations. As vital as all of these subjects are, there is still more.

CAPABILITIES OF THE MIND

Your mind is capable of much more than we normally use it for, and it is our most powerful possession. Over 80% of the material stored in your mind is in the subconscious portion. Not very many people realize how much the subconscious controls our lives. It functions automatically during every hour of the day. It can be compared to an unlimited storage in a perfect computer. It is filled with previously forgotten ideas, readings, and suggestions. Like any computer, though, it is only as good as the person putting the information in - **the programmer**. That's **YOU**. Occasionally, we all must reprogram our subconscious to keep it up to date. This is easily accomplished by a form of hypnosis.

SELF-HYPNOSIS

"Hypnosis?" You say! "Has this guy flipped his lid? Now he wants me to go out and get hypnotized!" Not exactly.

What I am referring to is a form of self-hypnosis stage that every one of us passes through each day, just before falling asleep, upon waking up in the morning, and during times of extreme relaxation. During this time, your normally uncooperative mind is not being used and ideas/suggestions are easily implanted in the subconscious mind. This is the opportune time for you to introduce positive suggestions toward your study, review, and attitude toward your advancement in the Navy. It is during this "relaxation period" that your subconscious is most ready to receive positive suggestions concerning tests, or any other subject.

Think about it. If you are angry just before you go to sleep, you usually have a restless sleep that evening. If you wake up in a foul mood, the feeling normally carries over into a large portion of the day. You don't just "wake up on the wrong side of the bed." Your subconscious mind plays this trick on you.

POSITIVE SUGGESTIONS

The suggestions you place into your subconscious can be used as a reinforcement tool to affect your thoughts or performance in reaching any goal. In order to be effective, these suggestions should be kept short, positive, and in the present tense. For example, you should say "I use my time efficiently while I study for exams" instead of "I didn't waste my time while studying last night." Speak to your subconscious positively; not in a negative tone.

Don't treat these opportunities as a case of "lying" to yourself. You are using your power of choice to reprogram your subconscious. Your subconscious does not know the difference, and will accept anything you introduce into it. Therefore, if you repeatedly state, "I study efficiently" or "I concentrate and perform well on exams," you will find your mind accepting that idea as truth, and you will soon be more efficient in your studies, and more effective on exams.

VISUALIZE YOUR GOAL

Besides the act of affirming your belief within your subconscious, you should also visualize yourself accomplishing the sought-after goal. See yourself getting advanced. Feel the excitement and joy of placing a new "crow" on your left arm. To some this idea will seem far-fetched, but, believe it or not, this will speed up the attainment and realization of your advancement goals.

EXAMPLE OBJECTIVE STATEMENTS

Everyone should have an idea of what objective they would like to achieve in any given situation. You may have already established your goals concerning advancement in the Navy. Positive statements to program your subconscious should be repeated while your body is in a most relaxed state, and preferably after you have located a secluded, quiet atmosphere.

On the following pages, you will find some of the more common objectives, along with corresponding positive statements you may use to reprogram your subconscious. These may help to change both your **attitude** and **performance**.

OBJECTIVE: BETTER MEMORY SKILLS

POSITIVE STATEMENTS:

* I have a perfect memory and enjoy remembering information.

* My memory improves each day, and I am constantly more aware of my surroundings.

* I retain material that I read with ease and completeness.

* Whenever I need information, it comes to me instantly through perfect recall.

OBJECTIVE: BETTER CONCENTRATION

POSITIVE STATEMENTS:

* I have the ability to easily concentrate on any subject.

* My mind automatically blocks out all distractions while I am concentrating.

* My concentration always remains in focus on the subject at hand.

* Noises are only normal sounds from my environment, and they help to increase my concentration level.

OBJECTIVE: EFFECTIVE STUDY SKILLS

POSITIVE STATEMENTS:

* I enjoy studying. I look forward to studying each day.

* I am always enthusiastic while reading, and I find all subjects interesting.

* I form main ideas and complete pictures of technical information easily in my mind.

* I constantly review studied material thoroughly with total understanding.

* I read all manuals, publications, and directives with excellent comprehension.

OBJECTIVE: IMPROVED TEST-TAKING ABILITY

POSITIVE STATEMENTS:

* I enjoy taking tests. They provide me the opportunity to exhibit my knowledge of the subject.

* I thoroughly prepare myself for each test. I review all notes, texts, and related material. I easily memorize technical info.

* Correct answers come to my mind instantly. My answers are clear-cut and true because of my extensive preparation.

* I am confident and relaxed at exam time. I am a successful test-taker.

OBJECTIVE: INCREASED CONFIDENCE LEVEL

POSITIVE STATEMENTS:

* I am a talented, capable person, and I like myself the way I am.

* I have an unlimited potential in my chosen field of endeavor. My shipmates appreciate my talents and abilities.

* I am a successful person. My superiors count on my talents because they believe in me.

* I am a valuable asset to my division, department, and command.

* I believe in myself and my future. I am relaxed and confident in all situations.

OBJECTIVE: POSITIVE THINKING

POSITIVE STATEMENTS:

* I enjoy positive thoughts. I always make the best of any situation.

* I look toward the bright side of each day's activities. I constantly look for the good in other people.

* I am the best possible person I can be. I receive numerous compliments, and find compliments easy to give.

* I feel totally comfortable with other people. I am my own person, and deserve respect for my abilities.

* I can pass any test, because I know how to prepare for them.

DIRECTIONS FOR SUBCONSCIOUS PROGRAMMING

First, prepare your objectives and positive statements on a set of 3" X 5" cards so you will always have them available. You may use some of the statements provided on the previous pages, or make up your own. There is no limit to the number of positive statements you may use. Just remember to keep them short and easy to read.

You may not gain much from your first experience using this method. The secret here is repetition. Each time you try it, you will find yourself going into the relaxation stage deeper and more quickly. Some of the symptoms you may experience to let yourself know that you are in a self-hypnotic state are:

1. Physical relaxation

2. Arms and legs feeling heavy

3. Deep and rhythmic breathing

4. Tingling sensation in fingers and toes

5. Drowsiness and motionless

6. Outside sounds are meaningless

7. Time seems to pass quickly

SUGGESTED METHOD

Below is a suggested method for self-relaxation to program your subconscious:

1. Gather your cards with objectives and positive statements on them.

2. Find a quiet room. Sit in a comfortable chair or couch.

3. Read your positive statements.

4. Close your eyes and think of relaxing.

5. Deeply inhale, holding your breath while you count slowly to five, then exhale very slowly.

6. Inhale again, holding this time to the count of eight, then slowly exhale.

7. Repeat the inhale and exhale again, this time holding until the count of ten.

8. Now, starting at your upper body, concentrate on relaxing all major muscles. Relax your neck, shoulders, and arms. Think of your limbs feeling heavy. Continue the relaxation process with your chest, stomach, and legs. Relax every muscle in your body.

9. Visualize your positive statement, and the accomplishment of attaining each of them. See yourself gaining the successes you have just read on the cards. Feel the excitement of reaching your goals.

10. Slowly awaken yourself while thinking pleasant thoughts of happiness.

As you can readily see, this system is an excellent way to put "daydreaming" time to work for you. It can be done almost anywhere. The procedure is incredibly simple and rewarding. You will be making definite steps toward the attainment of your goals while improving your state of mind.

True success cannot be measured in material items gained, but in your true feelings about yourself. By reaffirming your objectives and positive statements into your subconscious mind, your confidence will assist you in gaining success in any venture.

This system can not only be used to improve your study habits or examination performance. It can assist you to be successful in your working habits, personal relationships, or even help you to quit smoking, for that matter.

ANNEX A

CAREER AND EDUCATIONAL OPPORTUNITIES

This annex is for your use as a reference guide of career and educational opportunities available to all Navy enlisted personnel. It provides a short description of each program and any special notes that may be applicable. If further research is required, you may find more information on the subject in the BUPERS or Transfer Manuals.

The reference guide is broken down into five areas: **Career Opportunities, School Programs, College & Commissioning Programs, Navy College Program, and Education Assistance Programs.**

CAREER OPPORTUNITIES

RATING CONVERSION

A program offering enlisted personnel an opportunity to convert to a rating which is more suitable for their interest or aptitude. This program also encourages members in overmanned or disestablished ratings to convert to an undermanned rating. With the Navy in the "downsizing" mode since the end of the cold war, several ratings will be disestablished or merged into other ratings. People in the affected ratings will be given an opportunity to train and compete for advancement in new ratings.

Normal Eligibility:

*Must be E-6 or below, and must request conversion to a rating that is not overmanned.

*Must not be serving in an undermanned rating, or in possession of critical NEC.

*Must satisfy all eligibility requirements for desired rating.

*Candidate shall not be currently serving in an enlistment or extension for which a reenlistment bonus was paid.

Reference: BUPERS Manual

OCS

Officer Candidate School provides officer indoctrination for enlisted personnel who possess a bachelor's degree or higher. Upon graduation, the candidate will be commissioned as an Ensign.

Eligibility:

* All enlisted personnel are eligible

* Must possess a BA/BS or higher degree

* Must be U.S. citizen

* Must meet age requirements as outlined

* Must be eligible for an honorable discharge

Reference: BUPERS MANUAL

CHIEF WARRANT OFFICER

Provides selected Chief Petty Officers an opportunity for appointment to CWO status for performance in the technical field similar to their former enlisted rating groups.

Eligibility:

* Must be serving in pay grades E-7 through E-9 on active duty

* Must meet minimum/maximum years service as of 1 July of the year of application. (Normally at least 12 years active duty and no more than 24 years...consult reference)

* Must be U.S. citizen

* Must posses a high school diploma/GED certificate, or service-accepted equivalent.

* Must be physically qualified.

Reference: BUPERS Manual

LIMITED DUTY OFFICER

The LDO program offers an opportunity for an appointment to regular commissioned status for enlisted personnel. Selection is based on performance in the enlisted rating group.

Eligibility:

* Must be U.S. citizen

* Must possess a high school diploma/GED certificate, or service accepted equivalent.

* Must have served in pay grade E-6 for at least a year, or be at least E-7 on active duty.

* Must meet total active duty service requirement (check reference) as of 1 July on the year of application.

* Must be physically qualified for a commission in the U.S. Navy

NOTE: All selectees are appointed to Ensign, United States Navy (or USNR)

Reference: BUPERS Manual

AVIATION PROGRAMS

These programs offer a commissioning opportunity to enlisted personnel interested in becoming Naval Aviators, Naval Flight Officers (NFO), or Intelligence Officers.

Eligibility:

* Must be on active duty

* Must meet minimum required test scores on the Aviation Selection Text Battery (ASTB)

* Must possess a BA/BS degree

* Must have at least 6 months obligated service remaining on current enlistment

* Must be eligible for an honorable discharge from service

* Must meet age requirements

NOTE: Selectees are sent to Pensacola for officer indoctrination and pre-flight training.

Reference: BUPERS MANUAL

CHIEF WARRANT OFFICER PHYSICIANS ASSISTANT

This program provides selected Hospital Corpsmen the opportunity for CWO appointment as non-physician primary health care personnel, trained to act as an extension to the Navy Health Care System.

Eligibility:

* Must be a U.S. citizen with a high school diploma or service accepted equivalent
* Must be in pay grades E-5 through E-9 in the Hospital Corpsman rating on active duty, with at least 6 years active Navy service, and not more than 24 years service by the date of commissioning
* Be a graduate of Advanced Hospital Corps School, Medical Service Technician School, or Nuclear Submarine Medicine Technician School
* Must be physically qualified

Note:
* Selectees will retain their permanent enlisted status while in the CWO Physicians Assistant Training Program. At graduation, the selectee will be appointed a Chief Warrant Officer, W-2.

Reference: BUPERS Manual

MEDICAL SERVICE CORPS

The Medical Service Corps of the Naval Reserve is available to qualified enlisted personnel both on active and inactive duty. The program leads to an appointment to commissioned status in various sections.

Eligibility:

* Must be on active or inactive duty
* Must be a U. S. citizen
* Must meet age and professional requirements.

Notes:

* Selectees will be given an appointment of Ensign, Lieutenant Junior Grade, or Lieutenant, depending upon the number of years of education and professional experience.
Reference: BUPERS Manual

SCHOOL PROGRAMS

A" SCHOOL
Class "A" Schools teach the fundamentals of specific ratings and the skills required to perform at the lower pay grades. "Striker" identification is gained through graduation from any "A" School. In certain cases, it is possible for a candidate to be advanced to E-4 upon graduation from "A" School.

Eligibility:

* Must meet normal entrance requirements of the school requested

*" A" Schools are normally open to personnel in pay grades E-1 through E-3.

Note:

* Depending on the length of schooling, and the choice of accelerated advancement to E-4, an extra active duty obligation may be required.

Reference: Transfer Manual

"C" SCHOOL
These schools offer advanced technical training required for more senior pay grades within a specific rating. A "C" School can increase a candidate's chances of advancement due to the advanced training available. Many personnel request "C" Schools as reenlistment incentives.

Eligibility:

* Open to E-4 through E-7, and E-3 personnel who are identified as strikers

* Must have 12 months on board present command

* Must meet entrance requirements for school requested

STAR

The *Selective Training and Reenlistment Program* provides first-term eligible Navy personnel with a guaranteed basic and advanced school, plus possible automatic advancement to E-5 upon completion of the Class "C" school, as long as the candidate is otherwise eligible for advancement.

Eligibility:

* Personnel eligible include E-3 strikers, E-4s/E-5s serving in certain CREO groups or in a critical NEC.

* Must have at least 21 months but less than 6 years continuous active duty, and not more than 8 years total active service.

* Must be willing to reenlist for 6 years

* Must meet minimum required test scores for the requested school

* Must meet appropriate performance standards

Reference: BUPERS Manual

SCORE

The *Selective Conversion and Reenlistment Program* offers assignment to a Class "A" school, and automatic conversion to a different rating, plus a guaranteed future assignment to a school of advanced training, if available.

Eligibility:

* Personnel eligible include E-3 strikers, E-4s, E-5s, and E-6s.

* Must meet required test score for school & have good record of performance

* Must have within 21 months - 15 years in the Navy

* Rate conversion must be from an overmanned rating to an undermanned rating

* Must agree to extend for the required training, plus reenlist after rate conversion occurs

Note:

* The school requirement may be waived by BUPERS if appropriate prior experience is documented.

* The RESCORE Program offers similar opportunities for conversion and re-training in a selected specialty to former members of the Navy who return to the service.

Reference: BUPERS Manual

SUBMARINE SCHOOL
The basic submarine course is located at the Naval Submarine School, New London, CT.

Eligibility:

* E-1 through E-6 personnel in ratings compatible to submarine duty, plus E-7 on a case-by-case basis, are eligible.

* Navy entrance exam scores must meet minimum requirement

* Must be physically qualified, and must demonstrate emotional stability and maturity

* Candidate must have clear record with above-average performance.

* Must be eligible for security clearance

Note:

* Candidate must be willing to extend or reenlist to meet required obligated service.

Reference: Transfer Manual

NAVAL NUCLEAR PROPULSION PROGRAM
This program is available to highly motivated and experienced personnel who will operate and maintain the Navy's nuclear submarines and surface ships.

Eligibility:

* Must be a U.S. citizen

* Must be eligible for a security clearance

* Must meet minimum Navy entrance exam scores

* Must be a high school graduate and meet age requirement

* Must meet high school/algebra requirements

* Must have a clear record and be physically qualified

Notes:

*" Nuke" training is available to E-2 thru E-6 personnel in nuclear-compatible ratings.

* Personnel must have a minimum of 4 years obligated service at the start of training.

Reference: Transfer Manual

COLLEGE & COMMISSIONING PROGRAMS

NAVAL ACADEMY
The United States Naval Academy at Annapolis, Maryland provides an opportunity for a career as an officer in the Navy or Marine Corps. Graduates receive a Bachelor of Science degree, plus a commission as an Ensign, United States Navy, or 2nd Lieutenant United States Marine Corps. Every year the secretary of the Navy may appoint up to 85 active duty enlisted people and 85 naval reservists to the Navy Academy.

Eligibility:

* Must be a United States citizen between the ages of 17 and 22

* Must be a high school graduate or equivalent

* Must meet SAT/ACT requirements

* Must be unmarried and have no children

* Enlisted personnel must have one full year of service prior to 1 July of year entering the Academy.

Note: Graduates must obligate for 5 years active duty. Candidates not initially selected for the Naval Academy will be considered for admission to the Naval Academy Preparatory School and subsequent acceptance by the Naval Academy.

Reference: OPNAVINST 1531.4

ECP

The Enlisted Commissioning Program provides the opportunity for a member to attend school full-time to complete a Baccalaureate Degree, and gain an appointment as an Ensign in the regular Navy. Outstanding enlisted men and women with previous college credits can complete degrees in 36 months or less through full-time study at NROTC colleges or universities through this program, drawing full pay and allowances while paying their own education expenses.

Eligibility:

* Must be a U.S. citizen on active duty

* Must have at least 4 years, but not more than 11 years active duty as of 1 September in the year of school enrollment

* Must have completed a minimum of 30 semester hours of transferable college credits (with grade of C or above) for a technical major or a minimum of 45 semester hours for non-technical major.

* Be at least 22 years old and be able to complete degree requirements for commission prior to 31st birthday

Reference: BUPERS MANUAL

EEAP
The Enlisted Education Advancement Program provides an opportunity for career personnel to obtain an Associate or Bachelor in Arts/Sciences degree in 24 months or less.

Eligibility:

* Must be a high school graduate or possess a GED certificate

* GCT + ARI scores must equal minimum requirement

Notes:

* Selectee is required to complete requirements for at least Associate degree

* Navy personnel receive full pay and allowances while attending school, but must pay for own education expenses.

Reference: OPNAVNOTE 1510 (updated annually) and OPNAVINST 1560.8

NROTC SCHOLARSHIP
The Naval Reserve Officer Training Corps Scholarship Program provides an opportunity to qualify for an Unrestricted Line Officer commission while attending college. If selected, an active duty person is discharged from active duty and enlisted into the Naval Reserve as a Midshipman for 6 years.

Eligibility:

* Must meet physical requirements

*NROTC scholarships are available to enlisted members under 25 years of age on 30 June of their commissioning year. Some waivers are available.

Note:
* More information concerning eligibility, application procedures, and available universities is located in the current NROTC bulletin.

Reference: OPNAVINST 1533.4

BOOST

The Broadened Opportunity for Officer Selection and Training Program prepares selected candidates for entry into the NROTC Scholarship Program or the United States Naval Academy. Depending upon individual qualifications, each candidate is guaranteed an NROTC scholarship or an appointment to the Naval Academy.

Eligibility:

* All male and female citizens of the United States on active duty are eligible. * Must be highly motivated to become a Naval officer Notes:
* Selectees will be sent to NTC San Diego, where classes begin each June.

* BOOST is tailored to assist motivated individuals who have been previously deprived of educational opportunities. Ambitious personnel whose high school records doe not adequately reflect their abilities are given every opportunity to succeed through the BOOST program.

Reference: BUPERS MANUAL and OPNAVNOTE 1500

SELF-EDUCATION – NAVY COLLEGE PROGRAM

NAVY COLLEGE CENTER

The Navy College Center serves as the Navy College Program's central location for receiving and responding to toll-free phone, e-mail, fax and mail inquiries dealing with all off-duty voluntary education programs. It provides easy access to "one-stop shopping" information on existing voluntary education opportunities. Its call center is open 7 days per week, 15 hours per day, staffed by academic advisors ready to answer questions. Call toll-free 1-877-253-7122 or DSN 922-1828 between the hours of 0600-2100, or mail request to: CO, Navy Education & Training Professional Development & Technology Center, Navy College Center, Code N2A5, 6490 Saufley Field Rd, Pensacola, FL 32509-5204.

NAVY COLLEGE OFFICES

These offices form a network of professional Education Services Specialists, Technicians, and Guidance Counselors located at installations around the world. These professionals counsel and advise Navy members on all matters relating to academics, tuition assistance, and also administer on-base education programs. Here are some of the ways Navy College Offices can assist you:

* Analyze and define your education goals/capabilities
* Review your previous college work and plan your future education and training
* Select courses that you will need to succeed
* Enter a suitable college or technical training school, either off-base or aboard ship
* Receive financial aid
* Obtain college credit for Navy training & experience
* Obtain and review your transcript (SMART)
* Review and discuss your rating "roadmap"

ON BASE PROGRAMS

The Navy invites colleges and universities to teach classes on-base at times most convenient for service members (normally at night and on weekends). Courses are offered at the vocational/technical, associate, bachelor, and graduate level. Completed course count for credit toward college degrees.

COLLEGE TESTING

The Navy College Office supports the Defense Activity for Non-Traditional Education Support (DANTES) exam programs for high school completion (GED), college admission exams (SAT, ACT), and college level examinations (CLEP). It also offers over 7000 college correspondence courses from many different colleges.

Personnel who are interested in this program should contact the local Navy College Office. A complete review of all courses/exams available is beneficial in determining the program which best suits each individual's goals.

SMART

The Sailor/Marine American Council on Education Registry Transcript (SMART) is now available to document American Council on Education (ACE) recommended college credit for military training and occupational experience. SMART is an academically accepted record that is validated by ACE. The primary purpose of SMART is to assist service members in obtaining college credit for their military experience. Information on SMART can be obtained from your nearest Navy College Office.

SMART contains:
* Military occupations held
* Military training courses completed
* College-level exams completed, including:
(1) College Level Examination Program (CLEP) tests
(2) DANTES Subject Standardized Tests
(3) American College Testing-Proficiency Examination Program (ACT-PEP) tests
(4) Regents College Examinations (RCEs)
* American Council on Education (ACE) recommended credit for each of the above
*"Other Learning Experiences (OLE)" – Not all training is granted credit recommendations by ACE. The OLE section of the transcript documents this training and includes reasons why not credit was granted.

EDUCATION ASSISTANCE PROGRAMS

TUITION ASSISTANCE
The Tuition Assistance Program furnishes financial assistance to all personnel taking off-duty classes.

Notes:

* Assistance is given for courses taken at accredited colleges, universities, vocational/technical schools, private and business schools and through independent study.

* Personnel may receive 75% of all tuition costs.

* High school completion costs are fully refundable.

* More information is available from your Navy College Office.

GI BILL

The Montgomery GI Bill program is for enlistees who enroll and incur a $100 a month pay deduction for their first year of active duty, but receive a great deal more (over $14,000) for college expenses. Depending on their enlistment contracts, this money can be used after two or three years of active duty while in the service, or up to 10 years after receiving an honorable discharge.

Congress always seems to be having a difficult time deciding just what our veterans deserve in the area of education after service to their country. Check with your Career Counselor to determine the exact benefits you are allowed.

ANNEX B

MILITARY REQUIREMENTS STUDY GUIDE FOR

PETTY OFFICER THIRD AND SECOND CLASS

The questions and answers contained in this study guide are broken down into pay grade sections. The first section should be studied by personnel prior to taking the Military Requirements Examination for PO3.

SECTION ONE - PETTY OFFICER THIRD CLASS

UNIT ONE - PETTY OFFICER DUTIES; LEADERSHIP

Who is the primary enlisted assistant to the Officer of the Deck in port?

Ans: Petty Officer of the Watch

What is the name of the official document which contains a chronological record of events taking place during a quarterdeck watch?

Ans: Ship's deck log

Who makes entries into the ship's log while at sea?

Ans: Quartermaster of the watch

Who normally makes entries into the ship's deck log on the quarterdeck while in port?

Ans: The petty officer of the watch

While in port, who signs the ship's deck log at the end of each watch?

Ans: The officer of the deck (OOD)

If a mistake is made on a ship's deck log, what procedure is followed to correct the error?

Ans: A single line is drawn through the incorrect entry, the correct entry is inserted, and initials are placed in the margin.

Where and when is the national ensign flown on a commissioned ship when not underway?

Ans: From the flagstaff at the stern from 0800 to sunset

What is displayed on the jackstaff at the bow of all commissioned ships when not underway from 0800 to sunset?

Ans: The union jack

On a ship with two masts, where would the national ensign be displayed while underway?

Ans: From a gaff located on the aftermast

What is the ceremonial hoisting and lowering of the national ensign at 0800 and sunset called?

Ans: Morning and evening colors

What pennant is hoisted five minutes before morning and evening colors?

Ans: The PREPARATIVE (PREP) pennant

What command is sounded immediately before the national anthem is played by a band at colors?

Ans: "Attention"

What command is sounded immediately after the national anthem is played by a band at colors?

Ans: "Carry on"

What is the procedure for hoisting an ensign to half-mast at morning colors?

Ans: Hoist it smartly to the peak or truck before lowering it to half-mast

What is the procedure for lowering a half-masted ensign at evening colors?

Ans: Raise it to the peak or truck, then ceremoniously lower the ensign

When, if ever, may the ship's commission pennant be flown at half-mast?

Ans: Upon the death of the commanding officer

What pennant is flown from a ship during the absence of an embarked flag officer or unit commander?

Ans: 1st substitute

What pennant is flown from a ship when the commanding officer has departed the ship for a period of less than 72 hours?

Ans: 3rd substitute

Other than at the United Nations, when is the only occasion that a flag or pennant may be flown above the United States national ensign?

Ans: During church services aboard ship, the church pennant is flown above the ensign

What bow marking appears on a boat assigned for use by a commanding officer or chief of staff who is not a flag officer?

Ans: An arrow

What bow marking distinguishes a boat assigned for use by a unit commander?

Ans: A miniature of the command pennant

What distinguishing bow markings appear on a boat assigned for the personal use of a flag officer?

Ans: The number of stars corresponding to the flag officer's rank

TRUE OR FALSE
Boats assigned for personal use of officers are marked with special devices at the peak of the flagstaff for the national ensign.

Ans: TRUE

What distinguishing device would appear at the peak of the national ensign flagstaff on a boat used by the commanding officer (grade of Captain)?

Ans: A Ball

What distinguishing device would be displayed from the peak of the national ensign flagstaff on a boat used by a commander?

Ans: A Star

When are side boys NOT paraded for official visitors?

Ans: On Sundays, or on other days between sunset and 0800, during meal hours of the crew, general drills, evolutions, and during periods of regular overhaul. NOTE: Side boys may be paraded anytime during daylight hours for civil officials and foreign officers.

TRUE OR FALSE
Side boys are paraded only for scheduled visits.

Ans: TRUE

As a section leader during the evening hours of a duty day, you report to

Ans: your departmental duty officer

To whom is the chief master-at-arms responsible to for the maintenance of good order and discipline?

Ans: The executive officer

Who usually performs such duties as holding reveille, maintaining silence after taps, checking sweepers, and maintaining order in ship compartments on a divisional basis?

Ans: The police petty officer (PPO)

What is the name given to Navy military police assigned to assist military personnel ashore?

Ans: Shore Patrol

If, while assigned shore patrol duties, you apprehend a military person in AWOL status, and he is in possession of a bus ticket to return to his unit, what should be your course of action?

Ans: Allow the person to proceed back to his unit on his own.

You are assigned shore patrol, and suspect a person in civilian clothes to be a deserter. The suspected deserter refuses to show you any identification. What is your next course of action?

Ans: Ask the assistance of civil police.

An enlisted member's performance evaluations determine eligibility for what medal?

Ans: Good Conduct Medal

Who may conduct a search of the body and clothing worn by a woman in the armed services?

Ans: Only another woman
TRUE OR FALSE

If you must use your nightstick to defend yourself while assigned to shore patrol, you should always strike at the offender's head.

Ans: FALSE

What is the term used for official information which has been determined to require protection against unauthorized disclosure in the interest of national security?

Ans: Classified information

What are the three Department of Defense security classifications?

Ans: Top Secret, Secret, and Confidential

What is the term used to describe a situation where classified information is disclosed to unauthorized persons?

Ans: A compromise

What is the security classification of information that, if compromised, could cause exceptionally grave damage to the United States or its allies?

Ans: Top Secret

Who may assign original Top Secret classification authority?

Ans: The Secretary of the Navy

What security classification is assigned to information that, if compromised, could cause serious damage to the United States?

Ans: Secret

Who may assign original Secret classifications authority?

Ans: The Chief of Naval Operations (CNO)

What security classification is assigned to information or material that, if compromised, could cause damage to the United States?

Ans: Confidential

Information that is not classified, but is reserved only for those personnel whose official duties require use of it, is assigned what marking?

Ans: For Official Use Only (FOUO)

TRUE OR FALSE
"For Official Use Only" (FOUO) may be used to distinguish certain classified material.

Ans: FALSE

TRUE OR FALSE
Combinations to containers holding classified material are changed each time a person having knowledge of the combination transfers.

Ans: TRUE

TRUE OR FALSE
You must have the required security clearance in order to change a combination to a container holding classified information.

Ans: TRUE

How is the security classification of a combination to a security container determined?

Ans: It is assigned the security classification equal to the highest category of material to be stored in the container.

How many times must the combination be rotated when locking a security container?

Ans: At least four times

A failure to comply with regulations concerning the security of classified material, but which does NOT result in a compromise, is known as a

Ans: security violation

What type of authority do petty officers have by virtue of their position in the Navy organization?

Ans: "General authority"

What type of authority do petty officers have by virtue of their particular billet held within the command?

Ans: "Organizational authority"

What publication gives petty officers the right to exercise general authority over all persons subordinate to them?

Ans: Navy Regulations (Article 0811)

TRUE OR FALSE
Extra Military Instruction (EMI) may be used as a substitute for punitive action appropriate under the UCMJ.

Ans: FALSE

TRUE OR FALSE
Extra Military Instruction (EMI) is never assigned on the individual's Sabbath and should never be used in order to deprive a person of normal liberty.

Ans: TRUE

TRUE OR FALSE
The commanding officer may delegate the authority for assigning Extra Military Instruction (EMI).

Ans: TRUE

TRUE OR FALSE

Except for major infractions, putting people on report should be done only as a last resort.

Ans: TRUE

What article of the UCMJ deals with the preservation of an accused person's rights?

Ans: Article 31

What could be the result if a suspect is not carefully advised of his rights and the opportunity to use them before he is questioned?

Ans: Self-incriminating statements may not be used in disciplinary proceedings. This could result in the entire case being lost.

How many personnel does it take to make up a full-strength squad?

Ans: 13 personnel

What is a section?

Ans: Two or more squads

Of what does a platoon consist

Ans: Two or more squads, a platoon headquarters, and a guide

In close order drill, a platoon headquarters consists of

Ans: a platoon petty officer and one or more assistants.

A rhythmic rate of march at a uniform step is called

Ans: cadence

How many steps per minute do you take when marching in quick time (normal cadence)?

Ans: 120 steps per minute

What is the number of steps per minute while marching in double time?

Ans: 180 steps per minute

When is the only occasion that a group of personnel may march in slow time?

Ans: Funerals

What order is given to cancel a movement or order started but not completed?

Ans: "As you were"

What degree of turn will be involved by a squad when the command "Right Oblique, March" is given?

Ans: 45 degree turn

At the commands "By the right flank, March" from the squad leader, which of your feet will actually complete the 90 degree turn to the right?

Ans: Left foot

When conducting platoon drills, and unless otherwise announced, at which side of the formation does the guide take his post?

Ans: The right side

If a platoon is not under arms, what is the single command used to dismiss the platoon?

Ans: "Dismissed"

What is a good rule to follow concerning your speech when conducting military drills?

Ans: Speak distinctly to the person farthest away from you.

When in a military formation, what position must the leader be in to give a command while not marching?

Ans: At attention

The "government" system found aboard U.S. Navy ships is called

Ans: the chain of command.

The art of influencing people to progress toward the accomplishment of a specific goal is the Navy's definition of

Ans: leadership.

What is the most important factor in leadership?

Ans: People

What should be one of your primary considerations concerning people when making decisions that affect a group?

Ans: Individual differences

What type of leadership are you using when you set the same standards for yourself that you expect from others?

Ans: Leadership by example

What does the term "moral courage" mean?

Ans: Standing up for what is right

A good leader makes decisions, good or bad, and accepts the responsibility and consequences for these decisions. What trait of leadership is exhibited by these actions?

Ans: Accountability

TRUE OR FALSE
A good leader performs the leadership and follower ship roles simultaneously.

Ans: TRUE

TRUE OR FALSE
Leadership and follower ship are opposites.

Ans: FALSE

What is the basic purpose of all communicating?

Ans: Understanding

What leadership skill involves starting new actions or plans without being told to do so, and being resourceful in completing tasks as assigned?

Ans: Initiative

Name two characteristics of goals set by effective leaders.

Ans: Realistic and challenging

What leadership skill involves breaking a job down into parts and determining specific steps to complete it?

Ans: Planning and organizing

What term describes the knowledge, skills, and behaviors that are used by the Navy's superior leaders?

Ans: Competencies

Which leadership and management category involves doing the right job at the right time in the correct manner?

Ans: Concern for efficiency and effectiveness

What leadership and management skill is used when a leader uses personnel available as fully as possible while assigning them meaningful work?

*Ans: **Optimizing use of resources***

What is a good practice in relation to job assignments when your subordinates are bored with doing the same job day after day?

*Ans: **Rotate job assignments to prevent boredom as well as to provide varied experience.***

What leadership skill are you exhibiting when you appoint someone in a work group to take charge of an assigned task?

*Ans: **Delegation of authority***

What is the purpose of a reprimand?

*Ans: **To teach***

TRUE OR FALSE
The benefit of a reprimand is lost if you humiliate the person in front of others.

*Ans: **TRUE***

The phrase "Lets work together to achieve the mission of our group" is an example of

*Ans: **socialized power.***

What leadership quality is exhibited by a leader's ability to hold back an impulse to say or do something inappropriate?

*Ans: **Self-control***

How does the use of socialized power make people feel?

*Ans: **Stronger***

Seeing the "big picture" to determine the cause of an equipment breakdown is an example of what leadership skill?

*Ans: **Conceptualization***

TRUE OR FALSE
Aggressive domination is an effective means of influencing subordinates to complete an assigned task.

Ans: FALSE

Persuasive speaking, putting ideas in the proper terms, and appealing to a "higher purpose" are examples of the use of what leadership trait?

Ans: Influencing

What is the key to effective "team building?"

Ans: Cooperation

What leadership and management trait is exhibited when a leader provides procedures, opportunities, and alternatives for actions which might be taken?

Ans: Advising

What leadership and management trait is used when a petty officer helps individuals to explore, understand, and discover solutions to problems?

Ans: Counseling

Having a strong conviction that others are fully capable of completing good work when given a chance is an example of what leadership competency?

Ans: Positive expectations

What competency of leadership and management is shown by the leader who is aware of people's shortcomings and realizes that all instructions will not be carried out effectively by others?

Ans: Realistic expectations

What leadership trait involves paying attention to and listening to a subordinate, and responding appropriately?

Ans: Understanding

When used in the Navy leadership role, what does the term "conceptualization" mean?

Ans: The ability to view a situation, identify what is happening, sort through facts, & draw conclusions.

What are the three types of courts-martial?

Ans: Summary, Special, and General

How many officers are required to conduct a Summary court martial?

Ans: One

Under normal conditions, how many personnel must sit in judgment in a General court martial?

Ans: A military judge plus 5 members

TRUE OR FALSE
A Summary court martial is a properly recognized United States court, and its actions are judicial in nature.

Ans: TRUE

What are the three types of "mast" used in the Navy?

Ans: Meritorious, Request, and Captains

PO3 UNIT II

NAVAL HISTORY, TRADITION, & CAREER DEVELOPMENT

When did the Continental Congress authorize funds to start building a Navy?

Ans: October 13, 1775

Seapower was an important influence on history as early as

Ans: 2500 BC

Who first implemented the use of galleys as warships?

Ans: The Phoenicians

What was the weapon used by the early galley warships?

Ans: A heavy beaklike ram

As in earlier Naval battles, the United States was able to defeat the larger Japanese fleet in World War II by the use of

Ans: tactics.

What were the Roman Empire galley warships with three levels of oars called?

A: Triremes

The Romans won the third Punic War by the use of

Ans: an amphibious assault.

During the latter part of the Dark Ages, the Venetians built a large galley warship powered both by oars and a single masted sail, and with small cannons for armament. What were these ships called?

Ans: Galleass

Naval warfare was changed by what major invention around the year l000?

Ans: Gunpowder

What was the name of the historic battle marking the end of galley warfare?

Ans: The Battle of Lepanto

Multi-masted vessels built by the Spaniards were called

Ans: galleons.

Who won the Battle of Lepanto (Oct. 7, 1571) between the Christian and Turkish fleets?

Ans: Christians

What was the name of the new age of naval warfare that superseded galley warfare?

Ans: The "age of sail"

After what year did countries begin building ships with more than one sail?

Ans: 1450

What country was the first to search for a water trade to India?

Ans: Portugal

What country financed Christopher Columbus' exploration that led to the discovery of America?

Ans: Spain

Early treasure-laden ships with warships as escorts was the first example of

Ans: a protective convoy.

What was one of England's greatest assets in the struggle for world power?

Ans: Its expanding Navy

What country was the first to mount cannons on the lower decks of ships, resulting in a broadside battery?

Ans: England

In the 1500's, the Spanish fleet was called

Ans: an Armada

The English defeated the Spanish Armada in 1588 through the use of

> **Ans: a combination of naval tactics and shipboard weapons.**

Who was the commander of the English fleet that defeated the Spanish Armada?

> **Ans: Lord Admiral Charles Howard**

What aspect of naval warfare became more popular after the defeat of the Spanish Armada?

> **Ans: Gunnery**

What two fighting concepts were included in the early English naval fire power system?

> **Ans: (1) Broadside fire power, and (2) ships maneuvering in the line-ahead position**

In what year did the American colonies begin their revolt against British aggression?

> **Ans: 1775**

What was the name of the first ship of the "Washington Fleet" sent out to intercept British store ships and transports in 1775?

> **Ans: HANNAH**

The date considered to be the birth of the United States Navy is

> **Ans: October 13, 1775**

Who is known as the father of our highest naval traditions?

> **Ans: John Paul Jones**

Who built the first warfare-oriented United States submarine in 1775?

> **Ans: David Bushnell**

What was the name of the first U. S. submarine made for warfare in 1775?

Ans: TURTLE

The first commander-in-chief of the Continental Navy was

Ans: Esek Hopkins

What was the name of the Continental Navy's first flagship?

Ans: ALFRED

Who was the First Lieutenant on board the ALFRED?

Ans: John Paul Jones

What was the location of the first amphibious operation carried out by the American Navy and Marines?

Ans: New Providence Island (Bahamas)

The first official recognition by a foreign country of the American "Stars and Stripes" was in what country?

Ans: France

Who exclaimed the immortal reply "I have not yet begun to fight" during battle with the British?

Ans: John Paul Jones

What ship did John Paul Jones command in a famous battle against the British frigate SERAPIS?

Ans: BONHOMME RICHARD

What situation caused Congress to pass "an act to provide a Naval Armament" on March 27, 1794?

Ans: Algerian corsairs were seizing American ships on the high seas.

Who was appointed as the first Secretary of the Navy on April 30, 1798?

Ans: Benjamin Stoddert

The United States fought a quasi-war entirely at sea during the years 1798-180l. With what country was the war fought?

Ans: France

Who was the commanding officer of the USS CONSTELLATION during a famous battle with the French frigate L'INSURGENTE in the West Indies?

Ans: Thomas Truxtun

What was the major factor attributed to the American frigate CONSTELLATION's victory over the French L'INSURGENT in the West Indies?

Ans: Training

In 1800, after peace was settled with France, what was the public sentiment toward the Navy?

Ans: Cut back in the Naval establishment

Each wartime period in United States history has been followed by

Ans: a reduction in Naval forces.

The brave Lieutenant who led the American raid into Tripoli harbor to destroy the captured USS PHILADELPHIA in 1804 was

Ans: Stephen Decatur

What war managed to bring new prestige to the United States Navy because of a few victorious battles at sea and on the Great Lakes?

Ans: War of 1812

How large was our Navy when war was declared with the British on June 18, 1812?

Ans: 16 ships and 4,000 men

What famous oak-hulled ship earned the nickname "Old Ironsides" during the War of 1812?

Ans: CONSTITUTION

What famous American closed off the British northwest positions by winning the Battle of Lake Erie in 1814?

Ans: Commodore Oliver Hazard Perry

The invading British were defeated in the Battle of Lake Champlain by

Ans: Thomas MacDonough

What was the name of Thomas MacDonough's American flagship during the Battle of Lake Champlain?

Ans: SARATOGA

What was the most important technological development affecting our Navy in the first half of the 19th century?

Ans: Steam-powered ships

What was the name of the Navy's first warship to use steam?

Ans: DEMOLOGOS (later renamed FULTON)

Who is known as the "father of the steam Navy?"

Ans: Commander Mathew Calbraith Perry

When was the Navy's first iron-hulled warship launched?

Ans: 1843

The Navy's first iron-hulled warship was a paddle sloop named

Ans: MICHIGAN

Who was the United States Navy's first admiral?

Ans: David Farragut

What was the name of the Navy's first propeller-driven steamship?

Ans: USS PRINCETON

The sailors who manned our warships during the Revolutionary War were primarily

Ans: volunteers from merchant vessels, whalers, and privateers.

What sort of restrictions was placed on our ship's captains during the Revolutionary War period concerning recruitment of new sailors?

Ans: They could enlist men for their ships in any part of the world.

The word "discipline" comes from a Latin word meaning

Ans: to teach.

In the Continental Navy, and in the early United States Navy, the common punishment for offenses such as desertion was

Ans: flogging.

When was flogging officially abolished as a means of punishment in the United States Navy?

Ans: September 28, 1850

Who gave the famous order, "Damn the torpedoes! Full speed ahead!" at the Battle of Mobile Bay?

Ans: David Farragut

The concept of punishment in the United States Navy is used as a

Ans: deterrent to repeated offenses.

When were the United States Navy's first uniform regulations approved?

Ans: February, 1841

Who is known as the father of modern naval ordnance?

Ans: John Dahlgren

What battleship was blown up in Havana harbor in 1898, becoming a major factor in bringing on the Spanish-American War?

Ans: USS MAINE

When was the rank of Chief Petty Officer established?

Ans: 1893

What was the name of the first operational submarine accepted by the U. S. Navy in 1900?

Ans: USS HOLLAND

What famous naval officer said, "You may fire when you are ready, Gridley" at Manila Bay on May 1, 1898?

Ans: Commodore George Dewey

Who was the Navy's first aviator?

Ans: Lieutenant T. G. Ellyson

What was the name of our Navy's first nuclear powered submarine?

Ans: USS NAUTILUS

What is the highest military award for bravery that can be given to an individual in the United States?

Ans: The Medal of Honor

In the time period between the Civil War and the Vietnam War, how many U. S. Navy personnel have been awarded the Medal of Honor?

Ans: 744

What is the mission of the Navy according to Title X of the U. S. Code?

Ans: "preparedness to conduct prompt and sustained combat operations at sea."

What is the basic designation of a conventional U. S. Navy submarine?

Ans: SS

What is the basic designation of a U. S. Navy ammunition ship?

Ans: AE

What is the basic designation of a U. S. Navy submarine tender?

Ans: AS

What is the basic designation of a U. S. Navy amphibious command ship?

Ans: LCC

What is the basic designation of a U. S. Navy destroyer tender?

Ans: AD

What is the basic designation of a U. S. Navy tank landing ship?

Ans: LST

What is the basic designation of a U. S. Navy guided missile frigate?

Ans: FFG

What is the basic designation of a U. S. Navy nuclear powered ballistic missile submarine?

Ans: SSBN

What is the basic designation of a U. S. Navy nuclear powered guided missile cruiser?

Ans: CGN

What is the basic designation of a U. S. Navy submarine rescue ship?

Ans: ASR

What is the basic designation of a U. S. Navy combat stores ship?

Ans: AFS

What is the basic designation of a U. S. Navy amphibious transport dock?

Ans: LPD

What is the basic designation of a U. S. Navy dock landing ship?

Ans: LSD

What are the six general rates that exist at the E-3 level?

Ans: Airman, Fireman, Seaman, Dentalman, Constructionman, & Hospitalman

When were specialty marks added to enlisted uniforms in order to distinguish between ratings?

Ans: 1866

What is the purpose of the Navy Enlisted Classification (NEC) structure?

> *Ans: To supplement the enlisted rating structure*

What does a Navy Enlisted Classification (NEC) code represent?

> *Ans: Special knowledge and skills that are not rating-wide requirements*

In what two ways do you become more valuable to the Navy each time you are advanced?

> *Ans: (1) You become more valuable as a specialist in your rating, and (2) you become more valuable as a person who can train others.*

What determines the number of people who can be advanced on any Navy-wide exam?

> *Ans: The number of existing vacancies.*

What publication lists required and recommended rate training manuals and other reference material to be used in studying for advancement?

> *Ans: Bibliography for Advancement Examination Study*

How often are bibliographies for each rating revised?

> *Ans: Annually*

How long must a Naval Academy graduate serve on active duty after graduation?

> *Ans: 5 years*

A qualification program in the form of written compilations of knowledge and skills required to qualify for a specific watch station, maintain a specific type of equipment or system, or perform as a team member within a unit is called

> *Ans: Personnel Qualification Standards (PQS)*

Each Personnel Qualification Standard is divided into how many subdivisions?

Ans: Four (1) 100 Series - Fundamentals (2) 200 Series - Systems (3) 300 Series - Watchstation (4) 400 Series - Qualification Cards

On what page of your enlisted service record are Navy service schools and correspondence course completions recorded?

Ans: Page 4

The Navy Good Conduct Medal is awarded for how many years of good conduct service?

Ans: Four years

After you are discharged from active duty with no disability, your SGLI insurance coverage will continue for a maximum period of how many days?

Ans: 120 days

What is the maximum amount of time that may be authorized for a special 4-day liberty in the Navy?

Ans: 96 hours

PO3 UNIT III

3-M SYSTEM; COMMUNICATIONS

What is the primary objective of the Ship's 3-M Systems?

Ans: To ensure maximum equipment operational readiness through efficient management of maintenance and maintenance support.

Who has the overall responsibility for ensuring that shipboard maintenance is accomplished in accordance with 3-M Systems procedures?

Ans: The commanding officer

Who is tasked by the commanding officer with the overall management of the Ship's 3-M Systems program?

Ans: The executive officer

Within the 3-M System, what does "PMS" mean?

Ans: Planned Maintenance System

Who screens, dates, and serializes all PMS feedback reports leaving the ship?

Ans: 3-M Coordinator

Who in the command is responsible for the coordination and direct supervision of all administrative aspects of the 3-M Systems program?

Ans: 3-M Coordinator

What does the term "3-M" mean in relation to shipboard equipment?

Ans: Ship's Maintenance and Material Management

Who serves as the principal 3-M Systems assistant to the executive officer?

Ans: 3-M Coordinator

Who has the responsibility of maintaining the job sequence numbers (JSNs) within the work center?

Ans: Work Center Supervisor

Who signs the quarterly and cycle PMS schedules prior to posting?

Ans: Department Head

Who must conduct weekly spot checks to ensure that required PMS is being conducted according to maintenance requirement cards (MRCs)?

Ans: Division Officer

Who establishes the shipboard 3-M weekly spot check system?

> **Ans: 3-M Coordinator**

Who maintains a current ship's maintenance project (CSMP) printout as a master copy?

> **Ans: 3-M Coordinator**

Who marks the status of work center PMS on the weekly and quarterly schedule?

> **Ans: Work Center Supervisor**

If equipment covered by PMS is modified, how does the department head notify the Naval Sea Support Center of the modification?

> **Ans: PMS feedback report**

Who ensures the departmental quarterly schedule is updated on a weekly basis?

> **Ans: Division Officer**

Who is responsible for scheduling weekly work center maintenance and supervising its proper accomplishment?

> **Ans: Work Center Supervisor**

Who has the responsibility of keeping track of a command's off-ship 3-M Systems training attendance?

> **Ans: 3-M Coordinator**

What is the purpose of the Planned Maintenance System (PMS)?

> **Ans: To standardize maintenance requirements on a fleet-wide basis.**

What reference document within PMS identifies the system or component involved, and provides a brief description of each maintenance requirement?

Ans: Maintenance index page (MIP)

TRUE OR FALSE
The "estimated time" for completion of a PMS action listed in the maintenance index page (MIP) includes the time required for assembling tools and materials.

Ans: FALSE

TRUE OR FALSE
The rate (skill level) indicated on the maintenance index page (MIP) is the minimum rate qualified to perform the maintenance.

Ans: TRUE

What does the periodicity code "W" mean within the PMS System?

Ans: Weekly

What does the periodicity code "S" mean within the PMS System?

Ans: Semiannually

What does the periodicity code "D" mean in the PMS System?

Ans: Daily

What does the periodicity code "Q" mean in the PMS System?

Ans: Quarterly

What does the periodicity code "M" mean in the PMS System?

Ans: Monthly

What does the periodicity code "R" mean in the PMS System?

Ans: Situation

What documents within the PMS System provide detailed guidance for accomplishing each maintenance requirement?

Ans: Maintenance requirement cards (MRCs)

When several identical pieces of equipment are covered by the same maintenance requirement card (MRC), what document is prepared to identify the locations of each equipment?

Ans: Equipment guide list (EGL)

To whom does the maintenance person performing PMS report completion or noncompletion of assigned maintenance?

Ans: Work Center Supervisor

Where are Category A PMS feedback reports (FBRs) sent?

Ans: Direct to Navy Sea Support Center with copy to the type commander

Where are Category B PMS feedback reports (FBRs) sent?

Ans: Type commander

TRUE OR FALSE
Category A PMS feedback reports (FBRs) are non technical in nature.

Ans: TRUE

TRUE OR FALSE
Category B PMS feedback reports (FBRs) are technical in nature.

Ans: TRUE

How are URGENT PMS feedback reports sent?

Ans: By naval message

How many different schedules are used in the planning and scheduling of maintenance actions?

Ans: 3 (cycle, quarterly, weekly)

What is always the first step a maintenance person should take in completing an assigned PMS task?

> **Ans: Obtain the appropriate maintenance requirement card (MRC) from its holding container.**

What PMS maintenance schedule presents an overhaul-to-overhaul view of planned maintenance actions?

> **Ans: Cycle schedule**

TRUE OR FALSE
Quarterly and weekly PMS schedules are made up using the cycle schedule as a guide.

> **Ans: TRUE**

Where is the PMS cycle schedule normally maintained?

> **Ans: Departmental office**

What schedule does the department head use to prepare PMS quarterly schedules?

> **Ans: Cycle schedule**

How are "at sea" days reflected on the quarterly PMS schedule?

> **Ans: By a line drawn through the appropriate days' tick marks on the schedule**

What schedule does the work center supervisor use to prepare his weekly PMS schedule?

> **Ans: Quarterly schedule**

How are uncompleted maintenance actions reflected on PMS schedules?

> **Ans: A circle is drawn around them**

How long are completed quarterly PMS schedules retained as a planned maintenance record?

Ans: 1 year

How are personnel assigned a maintenance action on a weekly PMS schedule?

Ans: By name

Who signs the weekly PMS schedule?

Ans: Division officer

What system provides for the reporting of corrective maintenance actions?

Ans: Maintenance Data System (MDS)

What form would be used to document a deferred or completed maintenance action on a ship that does not have automatic data processing?

Ans: Ship's Maintenance Action Form (OPNAV 4790/2K)

What form would be used to document a deferred or completed maintenance action on a ship with automatic data processing equipment?

Ans: Automated Ship's Maintenance Action Form (OPNAV 4790/2Q)

An ADP-prepared document that reflects a detailed listing of deferred maintenance actions within a work center is called the

Ans: Current ship's maintenance project (CSMP)

What form must be filled out by the work center supervisor to report a maintenance action that resulted in a configuration change of equipment?

Ans: Ship's Configuration Change Form (OPNAV 4790/CK)

What form is used to document all deferred maintenance actions?

> **Ans: Ship's Maintenance Action Form (OPNAV 4790/2K)**

Why is it so important to document all equipment configuration changes?

> **Ans: To ensure proper spare parts support**

What is the number of the supplemental form used to provide amplifying information relating to maintenance actions described on OPNAV 4790/2K forms?

> **Ans: OPNAV 4790/2L**

When using sound powered telephone procedures, how would you pronounce the numeral 9?

> **Ans: Niner**

What are the three parts of a sound powered telephone message?

> **Ans: (1) name of station called, (2) name of station calling, and (3) the message text**

When a sound powered telephone circuit is in use, and you have a more important message to transmit, what do you say on the circuit to clear the line?

> **Ans: "Silence on the line"**

What does the control station say on a sound powered telephone circuit to see if all stations are manned and ready?

> **Ans: "All stations, Control; Testing."**

If you are manning a sound powered telephone circuit on the fantail, how would you acknowledge receipt of a message on the circuit?

> *Ans: "Fantail, aye, aye" (Shortened version "Fantail, aye" also acceptable)*

How do you tell a station to repeat its message on a sound powered phone circuit?

> *Ans: "Say again"*

If a person on the after lookout watch is being relieved, how does he tell the bridge that he is passing the phones to his relief?

> *Ans: "Bridge, After Lookout; shifting phones."*

When the Repair Two sound powered telephone station has been off the line for the purpose of shifting phones, how does the talker inform Central that his station is re-manned?

> *Ans: "Central, Repair Two; back on the line."*

If you are on the sound powered telephone circuit in Combat and you realize you must exchange a faulty set of phones for a good set, what words do you use to inform the bridge?

> *Ans: "Bridge, Combat; changing phones."*

What sound powered telephone circuit designator is reserved for the Captain's Battle circuit?

> *Ans: JA*

Lookouts normally talk on what sound powered telephone circuit?

> *Ans: JL*

What is meant by the term "target angle"?

> *Ans: The relative bearing of your ship from another ship*

What is meant by the "position angle" of an aircraft?

> **Ans: The aircraft's height in degrees above the horizon as seen from the ship**

When reporting relative bearings aboard ship, what is used as the reference point (000 degrees)?

> **Ans: The ship's bow**

What is used as a reference point when reporting true bearings?

> **Ans: Geographic north**

Bearings are always reported using how many digits?

> **Ans: three (Example: "O90 degrees")**

What is the standard sidearm used by the Navy?

> **Ans: .45-caliber automatic pistol**

It is standard practice to load how many rounds into the magazine of the .45 caliber pistol?

> **Ans: five**

PO3 UNIT IV

HUMAN RESOURCES; SUPPLY

What is the purpose of the Navy's Human Resources Management Program?

> **Ans: To promote the effective use of all the Navy's human potential**

How does the Navy benefit by the use of Human Resources Management Program to their full potential?

> **Ans: Improved combat readiness and capability**

What Navy program guarantees every sailor a fair chance for advancement and greater career satisfaction?

Ans: Equal Opportunity Program

What are the results of good leadership and counseling?

Ans: Personnel   stability   and   improved communication

What Human Resources Management program helps to promote satisfying overseas tours for Naval personnel by conducting briefings on local customs in foreign countries?

Ans: Overseas Duty Support Program (ODSP)

What Navy program is set up to assist a member and his family to get settled in a new location through personal contact with other members of a new command?

Ans: Sponsor program

What is the governing instruction stating that the denial of equal opportunity to any individual will not be tolerated in the Navy?

Ans: OPNAVINST 5354.1

What Navy program emphasizes the rights of equality of opportunity and treatment for all, regardless of race, color, creed, sex, or national origin?

Ans: Equal Opportunity Program

What program ensures that equal opportunity exists at the unit level?

Ans: Command-Managed   Equal   Opportunity Program

Who is responsible for implementation of the Command-Managed Equal Opportunity Program?

Ans: The commander of the unit

What is the Navy's goal concerning drug and alcohol abuse?

Ans: Zero tolerance

What Navy instruction states that drug and alcohol abuse is destructive to Naval personnel and will not be tolerated?

Ans: OPNAVINST 5350.4

What are the two key elements for drug and alcohol abuse prevention?

Ans: Detection and deterrence

What clue could indicate that a fellow sailor may be abusing or possibly be addicted to cocaine?

Ans: Red raw nostrils

What person in the command is the contact point for commanding officers seeking assistance or information on matters regarding drug and alcohol abuse?

Ans: Drug and alcohol abuse counselors

What activity provides local assistance to fleet and shore commands in the counseling of personnel involved with drugs and alcohol?

Ans: Counseling and Assistance Centers (CAAC)

Which Navy program provides for the early identification of problem drinkers and drug abusers, and is designed to increase awareness of alcohol and drug abuse?

Ans: Navy Alcohol and Drug Safety Action Program (NADSAP)

What is the science of planning and carrying out the movement and maintenance of military forces called?

Ans: Logistics

What is the name of the system responsible for naming, describing, classifying, and numbering all items carried under centralized inventory control by the Department of Defense and civil agencies of the federal government?

Ans: Federal Catalog System

How many different types of stock and control numbers are used to identify and order material in the supply system?

Ans: 4 (1)National stock numbers (2)NATO stock numbers (3)Navy item control numbers (4)Local item control numbers

What is the most common identification number used to identify material in the Navy supply system?

Ans: National stock numbers (NSN)

A national stock number (NSN) consists of a 13-digit number. What are the first 4 digits of this group called?

Ans: Federal supply classification (FSC) code number

A NATO stock number is identical to a national stock number with the exception of

Ans: A national codification bureau (NCB) code

When a NATO stock number is being identified, what two national codification bureau (NCB) codes identify an American item?

Ans: 00 and 01

What do Navy item control numbers identify?

Ans: Items that are not included in the Federal Catalog System, but are stocked in the Navy Supply System

TRUE OR FALSE
Local item stock numbers cannot be used in requisitions being
sent out to order supplies outside the local command.

> *Ans*: *TRUE*

What is the purpose of the cognizance symbol in the Navy
Supply System?

> *Ans: To identify the inventory manager who*
> *exercises supply management over specific*
> *categories of material*

When ordering material through the Navy Supply System, all
items must be referred to by its

> *Ans: Official government name*

Where is basic management data necessary in preparing
requisitions found, including stock numbers, units of issue, and
unit prices?

> *Ans: Management List - Navy (ML-N)*

How often is the Management List-Navy (ML-N) updated?

> *Ans: Quarterly*

What publication contains a listing of mandatory turn-in
repairable items?

> *Ans: Master Repairable Items List (MRIL)*

Where would you find a complete listing of all parts required to
operate and maintain the equipment installed in each ship?

> *Ans: Coordinated Shipboard Allowance List*
> *(COSAL)*

How often is the Afloat Shopping Guide updated?

> *Ans: Annually*

What are the two basic methods of procuring required items through the Navy Supply System?

Ans: Requisition and purchase

What DOD system is the most common method of requisitioning materials?

Ans: Military Standard Requisitioning and Issue Procedure (MILSTRIP)

What supply form would a supply petty officer prepare to request material onboard a non-automated surface ship?

Ans: NAVSUP Form 1250

What document is prepared by a supply petty officer to request material on an ADP (automated) surface ship?

Ans: DD Form 1348

What are the two main reasons for using NAVSUP Form 1250s within the Navy Supply System?

Ans: (1) To improve inventory control procedures, and (2) to report consumption of material under the Maintenance Data System (MDS)

When requisitioning material with a DD Form 1348, what is the most important identification data for any item?

Ans: The national stock number (NSN)

What form is used to order certain materials (such as bulk fuel and security equipment) that are excluded from MILSTRIP?

Ans: DD Form 1149

In what publication would you find complete information concerning the preparation of Casualty Reports (CASREP)?

Ans: NWP 7 (Operational Reports)

What are the four types of reports within the Navy's CASREP system?

Ans: Initial, Update, Correct, and Cancel

What type of casualty report is sent to submit changes to an initial report?

Ans: Update

What type of casualty report message would be sent when a previously reported piece of equipment is repaired and back in operational status?

Ans: Correct

What type of casualty report is sent when equipment which has been the subject of casualty reporting is scheduled to be repaired during overhaul or by other scheduled availability?

Ans: Cancel

What type of requisition is sent out via message in support of a casualty report requirement?

Ans: Not Operational Ready - Supply (NORS)

You know that a part is failing in a piece of equipment, and there are no spares of that specific part on board. What type of requisition message should be transmitted?

Ans: Anticipated Not Operationally Ready - Supply (ANORS)

What are the three ways of expending material within the Navy's supply system?

Ans: Issue, transfer, and survey

What is the term used to identify the physical release of material by the supply department or division to the user of the material?

Ans: Issue

What is the term used to identify the movement of material from the custody and records of one activity to the custody and records of another activity?

Ans: Transfer

A piece of equipment at your command is condemned as a result of severe damage. What supply procedure is necessary by your command?

Ans: Survey

What is the most common document used to transfer material from one command to another command?

Ans: DD Form 1348-1

Why does the Navy "survey" material?

Ans: To determine the reason or responsibility for loss, damage, or destruction of material, and to determine the actual loss to the U.S. government

What military program has been established to help eliminate the trafficking of illegal drugs and other contraband into the United States?

Ans: Military Customs Inspection Program

PO3 UNIT V

DAMAGE CONTROL & SAFETY

What are the two major organizations in damage control called?

Ans: Administration and Battle organization

In any shipboard organization, who is responsible for ensuring the crew is adequately trained and continually exercised in all damage control aspects?

Ans: Commanding officer

Who is responsible for the general supervision of all phases of damage control aboard ship?

Ans: Executive officer

What officer aboard ship is charged with the overall responsibility for repairs to the hull?

Ans: Engineering officer

If a ship has an assigned fire marshall, in what department would he be working?

Ans: Engineering department

When entering a space aboard ship, where would you find information relating to the types of damage control fittings located within that space?

Ans: Compartment check-off list (CCOL)

Who has the responsibility of making sure all necessary inspections of division damage control equipment are carried out?

Ans: Division damage control petty officer

Who is responsible for ensuring that personnel within the Operations department are assigned to damage control, repair, fire, and rescue parties?

Ans: Department head

Who must ensure that safety precautions and operating instructions are posted in division spaces?

Ans: Division damage control petty officer

When a ship is damaged, what aspect of the damage control organization is responsible for restoring the ship to working condition?

Ans: Battle organization

In the damage control battle organization, what station receives and evaluates reports from all damage control units, and initiates orders necessary to correct damage?

*Ans: **Damage Control Central (DCC)***

What is the normal battle station of the Damage Control Assistant?

*Ans: **Damage Control Central (DCC)***

What is the primary purpose of Damage Control Central?

*Ans: **To determine the condition of the ship and the corrective action to take concerning damage***

On board ship, what numbered repair party will normally have responsibility for the main deck?

*Ans: **Repair 1***

On board ship, what numbered repair party will normally have responsibility for propulsion repair?

*Ans: **Repair 5***

Who is tasked with the responsibility of assigning repair party personnel to form an effective damage control and damage repair group?

*Ans: **Repair party leader***

What member of the repair party takes charge of all actions at the scene and directs the efforts of the repair party to fight fires, flooding, and structural damage?

*Ans: **Scene leader***

Who must ensure that repair party equipment is kept in the proper state of stowage and maintenance?

*Ans: **Repair party leader***

What member of the repair party is known as the primary investigator?

> **Ans: #1 OBA Man**

Who is responsible for rigging casualty power in a repair party?

> **Ans: Repair party electrician**

For what purpose would the materials in a shoring kit be used?

> **Ans: Patching holes in decks, bulkheads, and hull. Also used in preserving the strength of beams, frames, decks, or bulkheads.**

What is the purpose of an oxygen indicator?

> **Ans: To determine if enough oxygen is present in a space to support life**

What is the next step in procedure aboard ship if it is determined that the at-sea fire party cannot bring a fire under control?

> **Ans: General quarters**

How many hose teams are in each shipboard fire party?

> **Ans: Two**

What is the minimum number of personnel required to man a 1 1/2-inch fire hose?

> **Ans: Three**

Who sets the fire boundaries as established by DC Central?

> **Ans: Investigator**

What member of the shipboard fire party carries equipment necessary to open jammed fittings and locked doors at the scene, while clearing routes to gain access to the fire?

> **Ans: Access man**

What three components must be present in order for a fire to burn?

Ans: Fuel, heat, & oxygen

What class of fire is burning magnesium alloy?

Ans: Class D

What sound powered telephone circuit should the telephone talker of a fire party use to communicate with either DC Central or the repair party?

Ans: JZ Circuit

How many different firemain systems are used aboard naval ships?

Ans: Four

The pumping capacity of the P-250 firefighting pump is how many gallons of water per minute?

Ans: 250

What class of fire is burning gasoline?

Ans: B

What is the primary extinguishing agent for a gasoline fire?

Ans: Foam

What class designation is given to electrical fires?

Ans: CLASS C

What is the primary extinguishing agent for an electrical fire?

Ans: CO2

What class of fire is one containing burning clothes and bedding?

Ans: A

What color are fireplugs painted in a shipboard firemain system?

Ans: Red

What color are interior JP-5 fuel pipes painted aboard ship?

Ans: Purple

Why are arrows painted on shipboard piping systems?

Ans: To distinguish the direction of flow

If you are looking at a deck drain identified as being located at 3-105-1, what does the first numeral tell you?

Ans: It is on the third deck

In the example of a deck drain with location identified as 3-105-1, what does the center group of numerals tell you?

Ans: Frame number 105

If the shipboard deck drain is located at 3-105-1, on what side of the ship is the drain located?

Ans: Starboard

A compartment onboard a ship is numbered 2-20-1-L. On what deck is the compartment located?

Ans: Second deck

On what side of the ship is compartment 2-20-1-L located?

Ans: Starboard

When a shipboard compartment is numbered 3-20-4-L, on what side of the ship is the compartment located?

Ans: Port side

What material condition of readiness provides maximum protection in battle?

Ans: ZEBRA

What shipboard material condition of readiness is set while at sea, in port during wartime, and in port during peacetime after working hours?

Ans: YOKE

Once activated, how long will the emergency escape breathing device (EEBD) provide breathable air?

Ans: 15 minutes

TRUE OR FALSE
The emergency escape breathing device was designed as a replacement for the OBA.

Ans: FALSE

The hood of the emergency escape breathing device (EEBD) will protect your face from an open flame for approximately how long?

Ans: 6 seconds

Who is responsible for coordinating the implementation of a comprehensive safety program based on the commanding officer's objectives?

Ans: Safety officer

Who is the safety officer for each division?

Ans: The division officer

What Navy instruction outlines the objectives and scope of the Navy Safety and Occupational Health Program?

Ans: OPNAVINST 5100.8

What type of tag is used on equipment as a precautionary measure to provide temporary special instructions or to indicate unusual caution to be exercised while operating such equipment?

Ans: CAUTION tag

What color are CAUTION tags used in shipboard equipment tag-out procedures?

Ans: Yellow

What type of tag should be used to prohibit the operation of equipment that could jeopardize the safety of personnel or that could damage the equipment, systems, or components?

Ans: DANGER tag

What color are DANGER tags that are used in shipboard equipment tag-out procedures?

Ans: Red

In almost every case, bleeding can be stopped by what method?

Ans: Direct pressure on the wound

When using mouth-to-mouth technique of artificial ventilation, how often should you force air into an adult victim's lungs?

Ans: Once every 5 seconds

How much blood loss will usually cause a person to go into shock?

Ans: 2 pints

A burn that produces redness in skin, tenderness, and slight pain is classified as what degree of burn?

Ans: First degree

A burn that produces blisters, severe pain, some dehydration, and possible shock is classified as what degree of burn?

Ans: Second degree

A burn that destroys the skin and possibly the tissue and muscle beneath it is classified as what degree of burn?

Ans: Third degree

What heat exposure injury results from a breakdown in the body's sweating mechanism?

Ans: Heatstroke

What is the maximum height at which you can work on an unguarded scaffold without a lifeline?

Ans: 10 feet

How long should a fire watch remain on station after a welding job has been completed?

Ans: At least 30 minutes

What type of leave is NOT chargeable against a person's leave record?

Ans: Convalescent leave

MILITARY REQUIREMENTS FOR PETTY OFFICER SECOND CLASS

NOTE: While preparing for Petty Officer Second Class, remember that you are also responsible for the standards and information at all lower levels. Review all previous material in this guide to enhance your readiness for any Examination.

PO2 UNIT I

SEAPOWER; ADMINISTRATION

What was the purpose of the Merchant Marine Act of 1936?

> *Ans: To establish a strong merchant marine capable of service as a naval auxiliary in time of war or national emergency*

Before World War II, from what segment of society did the United States Navy receive most of its trained manpower?

> *Ans: Merchant seamen*

What Naval Warfare publication outlines our commitment to the security of the country?

> *Ans: NWP 1*

What branch of the U. S. military made it possible for the United States to send most of its war supplies to Southeast Asia during the Vietnam War?

> *Ans: United States Navy*

What is the world ranking of the United States with reference to the total number of merchant vessels?

Ans: Eleventh

When was the Military Sealift Command established?

Ans: 1949

Under what United States cabinet department does the Military Sealift Command operate?

Ans: Department of Defense

What two general ship categories comprise the Military Sealift Command?

Ans: Nucleus fleet & chartered fleet

Under what government department does the United States Coast Guard normally operate?

Ans: Department of Homeland Security

In time of war, the United States Coast Guard would operate as part of

Ans: The United States Navy

In what year was the United States Coast Guard first established as the "United States Revenue Marine?"

Ans: 1790

What service branch has responsibility for installation and maintenance of aids to navigation?

Ans: Coast Guard

What ocean is known as the "main highway of commerce?"

Ans: Atlantic

What is the most heavily traveled stretch of water in the world?

> *Ans: The North Atlantic*

Which of the world's oceans is the largest?

> *Ans: Pacific*

What is the main function of the United States Navy?

> *Ans: To organize, train, and equip Navy and Marine Corps forces to conduct prompt and sustained combat operations at sea.*

What nuclear-warhead missile replaced the Polaris?

> *Ans: Poseidon*

The "broad course of action designed to achieve national objectives in support of national interests" is a statement defining

> *Ans: National Strategy*

What is the mission of the United States Navy?

> *Ans: To be prepared for prompt and sustained combat operations in support of the national interest*

What term is used to refer to generalized conditions, frequently of a continuing nature, the pursuit or protection of which is perceived to be advantageous to the nation?

> *Ans: National objectives*

What are the two major functions that the United States Navy must perform in accomplishing its mission?

> *Ans: Sea control and power projection*

The basic function of the United States Navy is

> *Ans: Sea control*

What are the three main roles of the U.S. Navy in carrying out the functions in support of its mission?

> **Ans: *Strategic nuclear deterrence, overseas deployed forces, and security of the sea lines of communication***

What are the three main bodies of the Department of the Navy?

> **Ans: *The Navy Department, the shore establishment, and the operating forces***

What body of the Department of the Navy contains its central executive offices located at the seat of government and establishes policy for the other two components of the department?

> **Ans: *The Navy Department***

What is the function of the shore establishment within the Department of the Navy?

> **Ans: *To supply, maintain, and support the operating forces through the furnishing of required materials, services, and personnel***

To what unified commander does the Commander of the Seventh Fleet report?

> **Ans: *Commander-in-Chief, Pacific Fleet***

A destroyer in the Atlantic Fleet is under the operational command of

> **Ans: *Commander, Second Fleet***

A destroyer in the Atlantic Fleet is under the administrative command of what type commander?

> **Ans: *Commander, Surface Force Atlantic***

What type ships are designed primarily for the purpose of conducting combat operations by aircraft which engage in attacks against airborne, surface, subsurface, and shore targets?

Ans: Aircraft carriers

Heavily armed surface ships which are designed primarily to engage enemy forces on the high seas are included in what principle type?

Ans: Surface combatants

What type ships are designed for the purpose of transporting troops and their essential equipment to an objective area, and landing forces on and over the beach?

Ans: Amphibious warfare ships

What category of ships includes those that provide underway replenishment, direct material support, maintenance, repair, and general support to deployed units, forces, or shore-based commands?

Ans: Auxiliary ships

What fundamental warfare task includes the destruction of enemy aircraft and airborne weapons, whether launched from the air, surface, sub-surface or land?

Ans: Anti-air warfare (AAW)

What fundamental warfare task is defined as the destruction or neutralization of enemy submarines?

Ans: Anti-submarine warfare (ASW)

What fundamental warfare task is defined as the destruction of enemy surface combatants and merchant ships?

Ans: Anti-surface ship warfare (ASUW)

What supporting warfare task includes the assessment and management of information obtained via surveillance, reconnaissance, and other means in order to locate, identify, and determine technical abilities or tactics of the enemy?

Ans: Intelligence

What warfare task includes the destruction of enemy targets ashore through the use of conventional or nuclear weapons?

Ans: Strike warfare

What is the positioning of naval forces for warfare in sensitive areas of the world called?

Ans: Naval presence

What term describes the sum of the capabilities of the Nation to use ocean areas for its political, economic, and military activities in times of peace or war to obtain its national objectives?

Ans: Seapower

What type of requirements do Naval Standards encompass?

Ans: Military requirements

A petty officer may be appointed by the commanding officer to stand a watch which places this petty officer in charge of the unit. What title is given this petty officer while on watch?

Ans: Officer of the Deck (OOD)

When the commanding officer is not on board the ship, to whom does the officer of the deck make his reports?

Ans: Command Duty Officer (CDO)

Who gives boat coxswains their trip orders and their orders to shove off?

Ans: Officer of the Deck (OOD)

Who signs the deck log at the conclusion of a quarterdeck watch?

Ans: Officer of the Deck (OOD;

While acting as an officer of the deck inport, a PO2 is subject only to the orders of what individuals?

Ans: The commanding officer, executive officer, and the command duty officer

With the commanding officer's permission, the officer of the deck ensures the striking of the ship's bell denoting the hours and half-hours from reveille to taps. At what hours are eight bells struck?

Ans: 0800, 1200, 2000

What inport watchstander carries a long glass?

Ans: Officer of the Deck (OOD)

Who must be notified if the CDO relieves the OOD of his duties?

Ans: Commanding Officer

What document is a division officer's summary of assignments of personnel to duties and stations specified within each of the unit's bills?

Ans: Watch, Quarter, and Station Bill

Who is responsible for maintaining a master bill for an entire ship?

Ans: Executive Officer

If the division officer makes changes to the Watch, Quarter, and Station Bill, who must approve these changes?

Ans: Executive Officer

Who is responsible for maintaining detailed bills for the personnel in each division?

Ans: Division Officer

Each person on board a ship is assigned a billet number. What does the first numeral of the billet number indicate?

Ans: The person's division

What division is normally formed aboard ship to handle the indoctrination of personnel who recently checked aboard the command?

Ans: I Division

What service representative has the primary responsibility of maintaining good order and discipline aboard a ship?

Ans: Chief Master-at-Arms

What is the primary objective of any training given to naval personnel?

Ans: To improve combat readiness

What type of statements are occupational standards?

Ans: Task statements

What type of requirements are Naval standards?

Ans: Knowledge requirements

How many skills can a person normally learn at one time?

Ans: One

When instructing by oral presentation, what is the best method of checking trainee comprehension of the subject matter?

Ans: Oral questioning

What is the major prerequisite to the student learning process?

Ans: The student must want to learn

What is the term used for a device or piece of equipment pertinent to the subject of a lesson that is used to assist the student understand and learn?

Ans: Training aid

What is the maximum number of ideas that should be presented with the use of any one training aid?

Ans: One

An effective training method in which exact physical procedures can be shown in a step-by-step manner is called the

Ans: demonstration-performance method.

What is the true measurement of an effective shipboard training program?

Ans: Performance

In the direct demonstration (teaching by doing) method of instruction, what is the first step in the order of presentation?

Ans: Instructor performs and tells

In the direct demonstration (teaching by doing) method of instruction, what is the final step in the order of presentation?

Ans: Trainee performs under supervision

After you have taught a trainee a new skill, when is the best time for initial application by the trainee?

Ans: Immediately

Who prepares the ship's quarterly training schedule?

Ans: Command training officer

Who is the chairman of a command's planning board for training?

Ans: Executive Officer

What element of training must be incorporated as the keystone program for unit watch-station or work-center qualifications?

Ans: Personnel Qualification Standards (PQS)

Who assigns the specific qualification goals to be met by each individual involved in PQS?

Ans: Division officer

What is the title given to an individual who trains personnel and signs off completed training in the PQS package?

Ans: Qualification Petty Officer

PO2 UNIT II

NAVAL ORGANIZATION, LEADERSHIP & PROFESSIONAL DEVELOPMENT

What date is commonly regarded as the "birthday" of the United States Navy?

Ans: October 13, 1775

Who was named as our first Secretary of Defense when the department was formed in 1947?

Ans: James V. Forrestal

What is the largest government agency in the United States?

Ans: Department of Defense

What body of individuals acts as the principal military advisors to the President and the National Security Council?

Ans: Joint Chiefs of Staff

What is the main distinction between a unified and a specified command?

> **Ans: A unified command is composed of two or more services while a specified command normally consists of forces from one service.**

In the chain of command, to whom does the Secretary of the Navy report?

> **Ans: Secretary of Defense**

What office within the Navy Department provides legal advice and guidance to the Secretary of the Navy and executive assistants?

> **Ans: Office of the General Counsel of the Navy**

What office assures a prompt and accurate flow of information to the news media for the Department of the Navy?

> **Ans: Office of Information**

What office supervises the administration of military justice throughout the Department of the Navy?

> **Ans: Office of the Judge Advocate General**

Who acts as the primary enlisted advisor to the Chief of Naval Operations?

> **Ans: Master Chief Petty Officer of the Navy**

What officer has the responsibility of directing the procurement, distribution, administration, and career motivation of all Navy personnel?

> **Ans: Chief of Naval Personnel**

Task Force 77 would be part of what numbered fleet?

> **Ans: Seventh Fleet**

A task force is a subdivision of

Ans: a fleet

What is the first subdivision of a task force called?

Ans: Task group

Task Unit 60.1.1 is part of what task group?

Ans: Task Group 60.1

What is the basic unit of vessels by type?

Ans: Division

Under what shipboard department head would the main propulsion assistant work?

Ans: Engineering officer

The Combat Information Center (CIC) onboard ship is normally part of what department?

Ans: Operations

Responsibility for the total systems and material support in the Navy rests with what flag officer?

Ans: Chief of Naval Material

Task units and task elements are subdivisions of

Ans: Task groups.

How often should you assess your leadership skills?

Ans: Constantly

What leadership skill includes building team spirit, exercising self-control, and developing subordinates' potential?

Ans: Skillful use of influence

Comparing a work group's results with its purpose or mission is a means of determining

Ans: *effectiveness.*

Comparing the use of available resources to achieve results with a standard that assesses whether the job was done economically or wastefully is a means of determining

Ans: *efficiency*

If you total the number of hours it took to complete a job, you are checking the work group's

Ans: *efficiency*

If you look up the grades your division has received on inspections and the number of unit awards personnel have received, you are checking the group's

Ans: *effectiveness*

A leader who is a self-starter is demonstrating what leadership quality?

Ans: *Initiative*

A division LPO who establishes deadlines for accomplishment of tasks is demonstrating what leadership quality?

Ans: *Setting goals and performance standards*

Why would an achievement-oriented leader include fear of failure as one of his thought characteristics?

Ans: *He sets challenging goals.*

What is the most basic of leadership and management tools that involves decision making while selecting from alternatives?

Ans: *Planning*

What step in the planning process are you performing when you envision the end results of what you want done?

Ans: Establishing objectives

What step in the planning process are you completing when you think of other possible ways to complete the task at hand?

Ans: Determining alternative courses

What planning step is being completed when a supervisor adopts a plan of attack to complete a job?

Ans: Selecting a course

Who is responsible for the overall organization of the Navy?

Ans: Chief of Naval Operations (CNO)

What concept of organization is being used when every person reports directly to, and receives orders from one superior?

Ans: Unity of command

What concept of organization is being used when similar jobs or functions are grouped together, and every function of the unit is assigned to a segment within the organization?

Ans: Homogeneity of assignment

Ordinarily, a supervisor should be responsible for not less than how many individuals?

Ans: Three

What concept of organization refers to the number of people supervised by one person?

Ans: Span of control

How far should authority be delegated down the chain of command?

Ans: To the lowest competent level

What organizational concept occurs when each individual and group in the organization understands its goals and works together in harmony toward accomplishing them?

Ans: Unit of direction

What leadership skill are you utilizing when you have matched people and jobs to receive the best performance?

Ans: Optimizing use of resources

Your division is suffering from high absenteeism, waste, high accident frequency, and widespread complaining. What are these conditions indicating about the atmosphere of the division?

Ans: Bad morale

What leadership skill would you be evaluating while keeping track of work progress?

Ans: Management control

As a petty officer, what should be your first obligation to the Navy?

Ans: Mission accomplishment

What is the most difficult job of a Navy leader concerning people?

Ans: Controlling subordinates

To get good discipline, it should be combined with which leadership method?

Ans: Rewarding of desirable behavior

What leadership skill are you using if you motivate others to be efficient and effective?

Ans: Skillful use of influence

What type of supervisor considers all the angles before reprimanding a sailor for not following the rules?

Ans: Actionist

TRUE OR FALSE
As a general rule, it is not a good idea for a petty officer to reprimand a seaman in the presence of an officer.

Ans: TRUE

If you know about a person who is about to violate a rule, should you as a leader warn the person before, during, or after the violation has occurred?

Ans: Before

What is the first step in encouraging good discipline?

Ans: Get your subordinates to decide in favor of the desired performance.

What is probably the most neglected duty of Navy leaders?

Ans: Rewarding subordinates

When should a Navy leader give out the majority of awards?

Ans: Immediately after the act that is being rewarded

When should a petty officer reward poor performance?

Ans: Never

If a leader loses his self-control in a group situation, what problem is the usual result?

Ans: Loss of credibility

What type of behavior is usually emotionally dishonest, self-denying, and causes one to feel resentful and angry?

Ans: Passive

What type of supervisor behavior allows all personnel in the group to know where they stand and underscores respect for others as a rule?

Ans: Assertive

Advising a person in a primarily direct way is the recommended approach to solving what type of problem?

Ans: Disciplinary

If a person reenlists for conversion to critically undermanned rating, under what program did he/she most likely reenlist?

Ans: Selective Conversion and Reenlistment (SCORE) Program

What is the major goal of the Navy Campus Program?

Ans: To provide naval personnel with educational opportunities for meeting their career needs as well as the needs of the Navy

Under what program could a sailor receive financial assistance to attend college on a voluntary, off-duty basis?

Ans: Tuition Assistance Program

What program provides undergraduate courses of accredited colleges to naval personnel serving aboard ship?

Ans: Program for Afloat College Education (PACE)

What publication contains information concerning requirements and qualifications for special assignments, programs, and projects?

Ans: Enlisted Transfer Manual (NAVPERS 15905)

What is the most significant personnel management document located in your service record?

Ans: Enlisted performance evaluation

Who are you compared with when your performance evaluation is written?

Ans: *Others in the same rate and rating*

What does it mean when you have signed you performance evaluation?

Ans: *That you have seen it, and have had your rights explained to you*

Why does the Navy have a Selective Reenlistment Bonus (SRB)?

Ans: *To increase the retention levels of poorly manned ratings.*

What force is designed to be mobilized to supplement active naval forces in the event of national emergency?

Ans: *Naval Reserve*

What is the purpose of the TAR Program?

Ans: *To train, administer, and maintain the readiness of the Naval Reserve*

PO2 UNIT III

CHEMICAL, BIOLOGICAL, AND RADIOLOGICAL DEFENSE COUNTERMEASURES

What is the United States policy concerning the use of chemical or biological agents against an attacking nation?

Ans: *The United States will not use these agents first.*

TRUE OR FALSE
Nuclear radiation cannot be detected by any of our five senses.

Ans: *TRUE*

Who must provide the authorization for our military to use chemical weapons?

Ans: President of the United States

What is the term used to describe any process which reduces or eliminates the effect of biological or chemical warfare agents at a particular point?

Ans: Decontamination

What is the name of a drug capable of partly reversing the effects of nerve agents?

Ans: Atropine

What term describes the amount of biological or chemical agents actually absorbed by the body in a given period of time?

Ans: Dose

What type of equipment is used for detecting, identifying, and measuring the intensity of nuclear radiation?

Ans: Radiac sets

What term describes the intentional use of living organisms to cause disability or death to man or domestic animals?

Ans: Biological warfare (BW)

What is a pathogen?

Ans: A disease-producing micro-organism or microbe

Which of the nuclear radiation hazards will cause the least damage to personnel through contact with the skin?

Ans: Alpha particles

What are the four types of nuclear radiation?

> *Ans: ALPHA and BETA Particles, NEUTRONS, and GAMMA RAYS*

What chemical agents have physiological effects limited to the respiratory tract?

> *Ans: Choking agents*

Which of the chemical agent types are capable of producing serious injury or death?

> *Ans: Lethal agents*

What is the purpose of radiological decontamination?

> *Ans: To remove contamination and shield personnel who must work in contaminated areas*

What is the purpose of biological decontamination?

> *Ans: To destroy pathogenic biological agents*

What is the purpose of chemical decontamination?

> *Ans: To remove or neutralize the chemical agents so they will no longer be a hazard to personnel*

What is the most practicable way to accomplish rapid decontamination of shipboard weather deck surfaces?

> *Ans: Water washdown*

How many personnel normally make up a radiation-monitoring team?

> *Ans: Three*

What type of radiation readings does a radiation-monitoring team depend on to identify areas most in need of decontamination?

> *Ans: Gamma*

What areas are most important when a radiation-monitoring team is taking readings?

Ans: Areas that will be occupied by people

What would be the first symptoms if you swallowed a poisonous nerve agent vapor?

Ans: Excessive flow of saliva, intestinal cramps, nausea, vomiting, and diarrhea

What is the first action to be taken if your ship is under CBR attack?

Ans: Close up the ship

Chemical agents that produce temporary physiological or mental affects (or both) and render people incapable of properly performing their duties are known as

Ans: Incapacitating agents

What is the unit of measurement when discussing the exposure dose of radiation?

Ans: Roentgen (R)

What is the unit of measurement when discussing the absorbed dose of radiation?

Ans: Rads

What device measures radiation intensity, providing information for calculating how long personnel can safely remain in a radiological contaminated area?

Ans: Dose-rate meter

What device measures the total radiation received by an individual exposed to radiation?

Ans: Dosimeter

What two types of dosimeters are in use in the Navy?

Ans: Self-reading and nonself-reading

What percentage of nuclear contamination can be removed from the weather decks of a ship by the use of an effective water washdown system?

Ans: 85 percent

When decontaminating using a fire hose, how far from the hose nozzle should the water strike the deck?

Ans: 8 feet

What is an effective material to use when decontaminating water?

Ans: High-test calcium hypochlorite

What fittings should be closed aboard ship to prevent chemical or biological agents from entering the ship's ventilation system?

Ans: Circle William

Each ship should be stocked with enough impregnated clothing to support a minimum of what percentage of the crew?

Ans: 25 percent

What item is considered to be your personal first line of defense in the event of an NBC attack?

Ans: protective mask

TRUE OR FALSE
Protective masks issued by the Navy provide protection against carbon monoxide, carbon dioxide, and ammonia.

Ans: FALSE

A ship's crew at sea can normally accomplish what level of CB decontamination?

Ans: Operationally complete

What NBC agents normally will not penetrate a painted surface?

Ans: Biological

What nerve agent antidote is contained in personal decontamination kits?

Ans: Atropine

When treating yourself with the nerve agent antidote, how many injections may be given at ten minute intervals?

Ans: Three

What is the very first action you must personally take in the event of a chemical warfare attack?

Ans: Put on your protective mask

What item of apparel should be removed last when a person is getting ready to enter the shower at a decontamination station?

Ans: The protective mask

What color are contamination markers used to warn personnel that they are nearing an area with chemical contamination?

Ans: Yellow

What color is the background of a biological contamination marker?

Ans: Blue

A radiological contamination marker has the word "ATOM" painted on it in black letters. What color is the background of the marker?

Ans: White

What word is printed on the front of a chemical contamination marker?

Ans: GAS

ANNEX C

MILITARY REQUIREMENTS STUDY GUIDE FOR

PETTY OFFICER FIRST CLASS

AND CHIEF PETTY OFFICER

The questions and answers contained in this study guide are broken down into paygrade sections. The next section, plus the previous sections for PO3 and PO2, should be studied by personnel prior to taking the examination for Petty Officer First Class. All sections should be studied by personnel preparing for the examination for Chief Petty Officer.

SECTION ONE

PETTY OFFICER FIRST CLASS

UNIT I - PETTY OFFICER DUTIES; SAFETY

What Navy publication gives all persons in the naval service the right to exercise authority over all subordinate personnel?

Ans: Navy Regulations

What article of the Uniform Code of Military Justice (UCMJ) provides for nonjudicial punishment?

Ans: Article 15

TRUE OR FALSE
Extra duty can only be awarded as nonjudicial punishment (NJP) or as the results of a court martial.

Ans: True

Extra military instruction (EMI) will not normally be assigned for more than how many hours per day?

Ans: 2 hours per day

Normally, the authority to assign EMI is not delegated to personnel below what level?

Ans: CPO

What Navy publication contains an outline of the duties, responsibilities, and authority of division officers?

Ans: Standard Organization and Regulations of the U.S. Navy (OPNAVINST 3120.32)

To whom do watch section and work center supervisors normally report?

Ans: Leading Petty Officer (LPO)

What two basic types of duties are Navy people required to perform?

Ans: Military and administrative duties

On what document would a sailor look to find what duties are assigned to him in a ship's bill?

Ans: Watch, Quarter, and Station Bill

What ship's bill organizes the crew to handle the effects of such disasters as collision, grounding, or battle damage?

Ans: General Emergency Bill

What is the name of the official document which contains a chronological record of events taking place during a quarterdeck watch?

Ans: Ships' deck log

All deck log entries should be made in what color ink?

Ans: Black

Who supervises the keeping of the ship's deck log in port?

Ans: Officer of the Deck (OOD)

Who normally makes entries into the ship's deck log while at sea?

Ans: Quartermaster of the watch

Who normally makes entries into the ship's deck log while in port?

Ans: Petty Officer of the watch

Who signs the ship's deck log at the end of each watch?

Ans: Officer of the Deck (OOD)

Who submits the ship's deck log to the commanding officer each month for signature?

Ans: The navigator

From where and when is the national ensign flown on a commissioned ship not underway?

Ans: From the flagstaff at the stern from 0800 to sunset

What is displayed on the jackstaff at the bow of all commissioned ships not underway from 0800 to sunset each day?

Ans: The union jack

What pennant is hoisted aboard ship five minutes prior to morning colors and evening colors?

Ans: Preparative (PREP) pennant

When, if ever, may the ship's commission pennant be flown at half-mast?

Ans: Upon death of commanding officer

What pennant is flown from a ship during the absence of an embarked flag officer or unit commander?

Ans: 1st Substitute

What pennant is flown from a ship when the commanding officer has departed the ship for a period of less than 72 hours?

Ans: 3rd Substitute

What article of the UCMJ deals with the preservation of an accused person's rights?

Ans: Article 31

What title is given to the officer or petty officer who has been designated by the commanding officer to be in charge of the unit?

Ans: Officer of the Deck (OOD)

When the commanding officer is not on board the ship, to whom does the OOD report?

Ans: Command Duty Officer (CDO)

When weather conditions warrant, who is tasked with the responsibility of reducing the loading capacity of liberty boats to a safe margin?

Ans: Officer of the Deck (OOD)

To whom does the sounding and security watch make his reports?

Ans: OOD

When a ship's machinery spaces are inactive, men of the engineering force regularly inspect all spaces for violations of watertight integrity and for fire hazards. This is known as what type of watch?

Ans: Cold iron watch

When anchored under normal conditions, what is the customary scope of anchor chain to be let out?

Ans: Use a length of chain equal to 6 times the depth of the water

At what time are 8 o'clock reports taken by the executive officer or command duty officer aboard ship?

Ans: 2000

The Beaufort scale is used in reference to what condition?

Ans: Sea state

What circuit is the most important internal communications circuit on the ship, and should be the one most closely controlled by the OOD?

Ans: 1MC (Battle and general announcing)

What Navy publication is consulted for Records Disposition?

Ans: SECNAVINST 5212.5

Who serves as the commanding officer's adviser and direct representative in matters pertaining to security of classified material?

Ans: Classified Material Control Officer

An administrative determination that an individual is eligible to have access to certain classified information is known as

Ans: a security clearance.

What are the three Department of Defense security classifications?

Ans: Top Secret, Secret, & Confidential

Who shall be notified if classified material must be removed from the confines of the command?

Ans: Commanding officer

Who has the responsibility of taking precautions to prevent deliberate or casual access to classified material by unauthorized persons?

> *Ans: Every Navy member*

When a fabric typewriter ribbon is used to process classified information, how many times must the ribbon by cycled through the typewriter before it is considered to be unclassified?

> *Ans: Five times*

Records of destruction must be maintained for what categories of classified material?

> *Ans: Top Secret and Secret*

How long does a command retain the certificate of destruction for Secret and Top Secret material?

> *Ans: Two years*

What is the term for a security violation which has resulted in confirmed or suspected exposure of classified information to an unauthorized person?

> *Ans: Compromise*

What action is authorized with regard to classified material as a necessary measure to prevent its capture by the enemy?

> *Ans: Emergency destruction*

When official correspondence is signed by an officer subordinate to the commanding officer, what words must appear below the signature?

> *Ans: "By direction"*

Who at the command must sign any correspondence involving military justice?

> *Ans: Commanding officer*

What publication contains specific guidance concerning signature authority?

Ans: Department of the Navy Correspondence Manual (SECNAVINST 5216.5)

In what publication would you find an outline of the Navy's safety program and the safety organization?

Ans: OPNAVINST 3120.32

Where are recommendations from the Enlisted Safety Committee submitted?

Ans: To the safety council

What should you do if you notice an unsafe practice being carried out during your work day?

Ans: Correct the situation immediately

What Navy instruction outlines the objectives and scope of the Navy Safety and Occupational Health Program?

Ans: OPNAVINST 5100.23

Who is the safety officer of each division?

Ans: The division officer

What color are DANGER tags used in shipboard tag-out procedures?

Ans: Red

What color are CAUTION tags used in shipboard tag-out procedures?

Ans: Yellow

What type of tag should be used to prohibit operation of equipment that could jeopardize the safety of personnel or that could damage the equipment, system, or component?

Ans: DANGER tag

What type of tag is used on equipment as a precautionary measure to provide temporary special instructions or to indicate unusual precautions to be exercised while operating the equipment?

> **Ans: CAUTION tag**

What is a "job safety analysis?"

> **Ans: A study of a job to (1) identify possible hazards or potential mishaps, and (2) develop solutions to eliminate or prevent them.**

Name the four basic steps of a job safety analysis.

> **Ans: (1) Select the job to analyze, (2) Break down the job into steps, (3) Identify hazards or potential mishaps, & (4) Develop solutions to prevent hazards/potential mishaps.**

What enlisted body of individuals makes recommendations concerning the command safety program?

> **Ans: The command's Enlisted Safety Committee**

What type respirator removes air contaminants by filtering or absorbing them as the air passes though the cartridge?

> **Ans: Air-Purifying Respirator**

What type respirator is used when insufficient oxygen is present, when the contaminant has no odor, or when the contaminant is of such high concentration or toxicity that a cartridge filter in inadequate?

> **Ans: A Supplied-Air Respirator**

What type of respirator provides protection in oxygen-deficient environments or other environments dangerous to life or health?

> **Ans: The Self-Contained Breathing Apparatus (SCBA)**

Who must approve all cartridges used in air-purifying respirators?

> **Ans: The National Institute for Occupational Safety & Health (NIOSH)**

When the work station's dry-bulb temperature exceeds 100 degrees F, what type survey must be undertaken?

> **Ans: Heat Stress Survey**

What type instrument is used to compute heat stress surveys?

> **Ans: Wet Bulb Globe Temperature (WBGT) Index Meter**

What is "heat stress?"

> **Ans: The strain placed on the body as it attempts to regulate its temperature as a result of any combination of air temperature, thermal radiation, humidity, air flow, and work load.**

What are the two basic requirements of an individual for "survival?"

> **Ans: The desire and ability to live**

What regulation(s) gives the senior person in a survival situation the authority to take charge?

> **Ans: Navy Regulations and Article IV of the Code of Conduct**

Name the basic elements of survival by using statements derived from the word "SURVIVAL."

> **Ans: S= Size up the situation, U= Undue haste makes waste, R= Remember where you are, V= Vanquish fear and panic, I= Improvise, V= Value living, A= Act like the natives, L= Learn basic skills.**

PO1 UNIT II

EVALUATIONS; TRAINING; SEAPOWER

What is the most significant personnel management tool available to supervisors in the Navy?

Ans: Navy Enlisted Performance Evaluation System

The management block (block 38) is provided on the Navy Enlisted Performance Evaluation Report for evaluating the management ability of personnel in what pay grades?

Ans: E-7, E-8, & E-9

How often must enlisted evaluations be submitted?

Ans: At least annually

If Petty Officer Schultz is on board the command less than 90 days when annual evaluations are due, and a true evaluation of his performance has been impossible, what must he receive as an evaluation mark?

Ans: "Not Observed"

TRUE OR FALSE
If a person is disenrolled from a course of instruction for disciplinary reasons, an Enlisted Performance Evaluation Report must be submitted at that time.

Ans: True

Who are you being compared with when your annual performance evaluation is written?

Ans: Others in the same rate and rating

What does it mean when you have signed your performance evaluation?

Ans: That you have seen it, and have had your rights explained to you

What pay grades receive scale grading on the Enlisted Performance Evaluation Report?

Ans: E-1 through E-9

Personnel normally have the opportunity to submit information they feel should be included in their evaluation. How should the individual provide this information?

Ans: By submitting an Individual Input form to the supervisor

Individual members are allowed what period of time in which to respond to adverse matters in their performance evaluation report?

Ans: 15 days

Where should a sailor submit a request to have a correction made or to remove an injustice from his service record?

Ans: Board for Correction of Naval Records

A petty officer first class (CPO eligible) is petitioning to have an injustice removed from an evaluation in his record. How long prior to the meeting of the CPO selection board must he have his request to the approving authority in order to expect proper action?

Ans: 90 days

What action is taken if it is impossible for a command to obtain a member's signature on an evaluation report prior to its submission date to BUPERS?

Ans: Forward the evaluation with a cover letter explaining the circumstances.

What evaluation trait would be assessing the extent to which an individual can be depended upon to perform tasks, and his ability to ensure timely completion of assigned jobs?

Ans: Reliability

What evaluation trait is being reviewed when you are considering a member's ability to work successfully with subordinates, peers, and superiors?

Ans: Human Relations including Equal Opportunity

What evaluation trait are you reviewing when you consider an individual's ability to act independently and without specific direction while exercising good judgment?

Ans: Initiative

What evaluation trait is being reviewed when you consider a member's personal appearance including physical fitness, wearing of the uniform, and neatness in civilian attire?

Ans: Military Bearing

What three areas should you consider when assessing a subordinate's performance?

Ans: Attitude, Knowledge, and Work Habits

What should be the primary goal of the division training program?

Ans: To qualify people in the skills required by the command

What should be the secondary goal of division training?

Ans: Advancement and general military/professional training

What are the most effective type training lessons in terms of frequency and length?

Ans: Short sessions on a frequent basis

What method of training is being used when trainees are assigned to work individually or in small groups with experienced workers?

Ans: Apprenticeship method

What method of training is effective only for information that does not require a lot of "hands on" practice with complex processes or equipment?

Ans: Group method

What type of in-house training is designed to acquaint Navy personnel with their new organization, and their place in it?

Ans: Orientation training

What type of in-house training enables people to brush up on knowledge and skills they already have but don't use often?

Ans: Refresher training

What type of in-house training is not necessarily related to the trainee's jobs but designed to help them prepare for advancement?

Ans: Career or professional development training

How many skills can a person normally learn at one time?

Ans: One

Who is the sole person responsible for what is taught in a class?

Ans: Instructor

What is the major prerequisite to the student learning process?

Ans: Students must be motivated to learn

What are the three parts of the communication process?

Ans: Source, symbol, and a receiver

What is the maximum number of main ideas that should be presented with the use of any one training aid?

Ans: One

What variables must be considered when selecting methods and techniques of instruction?

>Ans: The nature of the trainees, the subject matter, and the limitations of time

What is the most frequently used method of instruction?

>Ans: Lecture

What method of instruction is used as a means of reaching a large group at one time with a condensed, organized body of information and with little interaction?

>Ans: Lecture

What is the primary requirement to effective communication?

>Ans: Receiver must understand the message

What are two effective ways that an instructor can check trainee comprehension during an oral presentation?

>Ans: Watch the faces of trainees and ask questions

After a new skill has been taught to a trainee, when is the best time for initial application by the trainee?

>Ans: Immediately

What method of instruction is an effective means of getting the trainees to think constructively while interacting with the rest of the class?

>Ans: Discussion method

In a true "directed discussion," the instructor should act in what capacity?

>Ans: Moderator or chairman

What is the best method of instruction when teaching skills in a step-by-step manner?

>Ans: Demonstration-performance method

What Navy publication contains complete descriptions and preparation instructions for training schedules and records?

Ans: OPNAVINST 3120.32 (Standard Organization and Regulations of the U.S. Navy)

What is the true measurement of an effective shipboard training program?

Ans: Performance

Who prepares the ship's quarterly training schedule?

Ans: Command training officer

Who is the chairman of the command's planning board for training?

Ans: Executive officer

What is the mission of the U.S. Navy?

Ans: To be prepared to conduct prompt and sustained combat operations at sea in support of U.S. national interests

Why does any nation maintain a military force in peacetime?

Ans: To deter the outbreak of armed conflict

What naval warfare publication outlines our commitment to the security of the country?

Ans: NWP 1

What ocean is known as the "main highway of commerce?"

Ans: Atlantic

What is the most heavily traveled stretch of water in the world?

Ans: North Atlantic Ocean

Which of the world's oceans is the largest?

>*Ans: Pacific Ocean*

What is the goal of strategic nuclear deterrence?

>*Ans: To prevent the use of nuclear weapons against the U.S. or its allies*

What three elements compose the TRIAD of nuclear forces which make up the United States nuclear deterrent?

>*Ans: submarine-launched ballistic missiles, intercontinental ballistic missiles, and land-based bombers*

When speaking of the deterrence concept, what is meant by "limited response?"

>*Ans: An attacked nation would retaliate with only enough force to stop the attack.*

What are the main reasons why naval forces are deployed?

>*Ans: To be in the position to engage the enemy promptly at the start of hostilities, to provide support to friendly nations, and to stop the advance of the enemy as soon as possible.*

What two basic functions does the United States Navy have?

>*Ans: (1) To be able to perform in a hostile environment, and (2) to exercise sea control and power projection*

What is sea control?

>*Ans: The capability of a nation to selectively use those portions of the high seas essential to their national interest*

During modern land warfare conducted by the U.S. Army and U.S. Air Force, how would a great proportion of supplies arrive to support the land troops?

Ans: By sea

What are nuclear responses by FBM submarines, the use of carrier-based aircraft and amphibious assault forces, and naval bombardment of enemy targets ashore examples of?

Ans: Power projection

The ability of the Navy to complicate the enemy's detection and targeting capability, and its ability to exercise the element of surprise is due to its

Ans: mobility.

What nuclear-warhead missile replaced the POLARIS?

Ans: POSEIDON

On what country did President Kennedy impose a naval quarantine to prevent deliveries of ICBMs in 1962?

Ans: Cuba

When was the North Atlantic Treaty Organization (NATO) established?

Ans: 1949

When was the Military Sealift Command established?

Ans: 1949

Under what U.S. cabinet department does the Military Sealift Command operate?

Ans: Department of Defense

Under what government department does the U.S. Coast Guard normally operate?

Ans: Department of Homeland Security

What service branch has the responsibility for installation/maintenance of aids to navigation?

Ans: Coast Guard

What is a "Type Command?"

Ans: An administrative subdivision of a fleet

What is the primary purpose of the command control that is exercised over a shore command?

Ans: Meeting the support requirements of the fleet

How many American Fleets are there to stand worldwide watch over the oceans?

Ans: Four (2nd, 3rd, 6th, & 7th Fleets)

Provide definitions of the following fundamental warfare tasks:

Ans: ANTIAIR WARFARE (AAW) - The destruction of enemy aircraft and airborne weapons, whether launched from air, surface, subsurface, or land.

Ans: ANTISUBMARINE WARFARE (ASW) - The destruction or neutralization of enemy submarines.

Ans: ANTISURFACE SHIP WARFARE (ASUW) - The destruction/neutralization of enemy surface combatants and merchant ships.

Ans: AMPHIBIOUS WARFARE - Consists of attacks launched from sea by naval forces and by landing forces embarked in ships or landing craft.

Ans: MINE WARFARE - The use of mines and mine countermeasures to control the seas and harbors.

Ans: STRIKE WARFARE - The use of conventional/nuclear weapons in the destruction/neutralization of enemy targets ashore.

Define the following SUPPORTING WARFARE TASKS:

> *Ans: SPECIAL WARFARE - Includes special mobile operations, unconventional warfare, coastal reconnaissance, and some technical intelligence ops.*

> *Ans: OCEAN SURVEILLANCE - The observation of ocean areas to detect, locate, and classify air, surface, and subsurface targets.*

> *Ans: INTELLIGENCE - The assessment and management of information obtained via surveillance, reconnaissance, or other means. Meaningful intelligence facts permit military decisions to be based on accurate knowledge of an enemy's forces or capabilities.*

> *Ans: ELECTRONIC WARFARE - Reduces or prevents use of the electromagnetic spectrum from the enemy, while ensuring effective use of it by friendly forces.*

> *Ans: LOGISTICS - Resupply of consumables to combatant forces*

Which shipboard integrated AAW combat weapons system is installed on all TICONDEROGA-Class cruisers?

> *Ans: AEGIS*

What is the mission of Surface-Launched missiles?

> *Ans: To engage and intercept aircraft, antiship missiles, and surface ships*

What is the name of the Navy's first all-weather, automatic-controlled gun system designed to provide defense against close-in, sea-skimming cruise missiles that penetrate outer defense systems?

> *Ans: PHALANX Close-In Weapons System (CIWS)*

PO1 UNIT III

PROFESSIONAL DEVELOPMENT

In what two ways do you become more valuable to the Navy each time you are advanced?

Ans: As a specialist in your rating, and as an instructor to train others

What determines the number of people who can be advanced on any Navy-wide examination?

Ans: The number of vacancies that exist

What publication lists required and recommended rate training manuals and other reference material to be used in studying for advancement?

Ans: Bibliography for Advancement Examination Study

How often are Bibliographies for each Navy rating revised?

Ans: Annually

On what page of your enlisted service record are Navy service school and correspondence course completions entered?

Ans: Page 4

What page of the Enlisted Service Record contains History of Assignments?

Ans: Page 5

What page of the Enlisted Service Record would contain a record of an Unauthorized Absence?

Ans: Page 6

What page of the Enlisted Service Record is reserved for Administrative Remarks?

Ans: Page 13

What page in an enlisted member's service record contains the Record of Emergency Data?

Ans: Page 2

What qualification program is in the form of written knowledge and skills to qualify for specific watch stations, maintain equipment or systems, or to perform as a team member within a unit?

Ans: Personnel Qualifications Standards (PQS)

How many subdivisions are included in each Personnel Qualifications Standard (PQS)?

Ans: Four

The Navy Good Conduct Medal is awarded for how many years of good conduct service?

Ans: Four years

After you are discharged from active duty with no disability, how many days will your Servicemen's Group Life Insurance (SGLI) continue to be active?

Ans: 120 days

What is the maximum amount of time that may be authorized for a special 4-day liberty?

Ans: 96 hours

When a person reenlists for conversion to a critically undermanned rating, under what program did he/she most likely reenlist?

Ans: Selective Conversion and Reenlistment (SCORE) Program

What is the major goal of the Navy Campus Program?

Ans: To provide naval personnel with educational opportunities for meeting their career goals as well as the needs of the Navy

Under what program could an active duty sailor receive financial assistance to attend college on a voluntary, off-duty basis?

Ans: Tuition Assistance Program

What program provides undergraduate courses from accredited colleges to naval personnel serving aboard ships?

Ans: Program for Afloat College Education (PACE)

What is the most significant personnel management document located in your enlisted service record?

Ans: Enlisted performance evaluation

What publication contains information concerning requirements and qualifications for special assignments, programs, and projects?

Ans: Enlisted Transfer Manual (NAVPERS 15905)

What is the reason for the Navy having a Selective Reenlistment Bonus (SRB)?

Ans: To increase the retention levels of poorly manned ratings

What Naval educational program provides self-study training packages of instruction in professional naval subjects?

Ans: Correspondence Course Program

What BUPERS Notice provides information for each regularly scheduled advancement examination cycle?

Ans: BUPERS Notice 1418

What happens if the number of vacancies in a given rate exceeds the number of qualified personnel?

Ans: All those personnel qualified will be advanced

What Navy publication should you consult for specific information concerning advancement in the Navy?

Ans: Manual of Advancement

What is the lowest pay grade that may request consideration under the Navy's Limited Duty Officer Program?

Ans: E-6

What must an "early" advancement candidate normally have in order to be advanced over "regular" candidates on each exam cycle?

Ans: A higher final multiple score than the "regular" candidates

Personnel who have been reduced in rate at commanding officer's NJP may have their punishment suspended if the commanding officer acts within what minimum amount of time?

Ans: 4 months

What pay grades are eligible to apply for the Physicians Assistant Warrant Officer Program?

Ans: E-5 and above

What are the two primary enlisted - to - officer programs in the Navy which do not require a college education?

Ans: Chief Warrant Officer (CWO) and Limited Duty Officer (LDO) Programs

How much education is required of candidates who submit for the CWO or LDO Programs?

Ans: High school education or service - accepted equivalent.

What is the purpose of the Petty Officer Quality Control Board?

Ans: To assist in the development and maintenance of a highly professional enlisted career force

Who manages the Navy's medical and dental training?

Ans: Bureau of Medicine & Surgery (BUMED)

What command is responsible to the Chief of Naval Operations (CNO) for most of the Navy's ashore training programs?

Ans: Chief of Naval Education & Training (CNET)

To whom is the Commandant of the Marine Corps responsible for the administration of Marine Corps policies and regulations?

Ans: Secretary of the Navy (SECNAV)

To whom is COMTRALANT responsible for conducting fleet operational training?

Ans: The Fleet Commander

Where do personnel in specific ratings normally obtain formal training at the job entry level?

Ans: Class A Schools

What type of Navy school conducts advanced training for specific ratings, and, in some cases, awards a Navy enlisted classification code (NEC)?

Ans: Class C School

What is the minimum size class for a course to be conducted using the Navy's Instructor Services Program?

Ans: 10 students

What Navy instruction outlines the Navy's Enlisted Surface Warfare Specialist (ESWS) Program?

Ans: OPNAVINST 1414.1

In what Navy program would a sailor participate in order to complete College Level Examination Program (CLEP) exams?

Ans: Defense Activity for Non-Traditional Education Support (DANTES)

Who is responsible for controlling the permanent duty assignment of enlisted personnel?

Ans: BUPERS

What determines how many people are recruited, what type of training they receive, and where they are assigned for duty?

Ans: Authorized billets

What are the three main functions of enlisted distribution management controls?

Ans: Distribution control, manning control, and assignment control

Who is the Manning Control Authority (MCA) for personnel allocations to the Atlantic Ocean area?

Ans: CINCLANTFLT

Who is the Manning Control Authority (MCA) for personnel allocations to most continental U. S. activities?

Ans: BUPERS

Who is the Manning Control Authority (MCA) for personnel allocations to the Pacific Ocean area?

Ans: CINCPACFLT

What Navy plan determines how personnel shortages and excesses will be distributed, and decides the most equitable level of manning for each activity?

Ans: Navy Manning Plan (NMP)

Who may direct priority 1 and priority 2 manning requirements within the Navy Enlisted Distribution System?

Ans: CNO

Where would you find a list of sea/shore tour lengths for all rates and certain NECs?

Ans: Enlisted Transfer Manual

What official means are available for a Navy member to inform a detailer of the member's desires for duty assignments?

Ans: Enlisted Duty Preference Form

What is the purpose of the Navy Enlisted Classification (NEC) structure?

Ans: To supplement the enlisted rating structure

What does a Navy Enlisted Classification (NEC) code represent?

Ans: Special knowledge and skills that are not rating-wide requirements

How many Navy Enlisted Classification (NEC) codes may an enlisted member earn and have documented in the master tape at BUPERS?

Ans: Five

What plan provides Navy members with the opportunity to leave a portion of their retirement pay to their survivors?

Ans: Survivor's Benefit Plan (SBP)

What happens to Survivor's Benefit Plan (SBP) coverage if the Navy member declines coverage under the Survival Benefit Plan?

Ans: The member's spouse must sign a spousal concurrence statement

What is the maximum annuity amount election that can be selected in SBP coverage?

Ans: 55 percent of full base amount

A spouse is collecting Dependency and Indemnity Compensation (DIC) payments due to the death of her service member husband. What happens to her DIC payments when she remarries?

Ans: The payments stop

TRUE OR FALSE
A retired Navy member who reaches age 65 and is NOT eligible for benefits under the Social Security system remains eligible for CHAMPUS benefits.

Ans: True

What medical plan do military retirees eligible for CHAMPUS normally become eligible for at age 65?

Ans: MEDICARE

If an available military facility cannot provide required inpatient care, what document should a military dependent receive from the military facility to ensure CHAMPUS payment?

Ans: Nonavailability statement

What agency helps the commanding officer investigate and verify facts surrounding emergency situations where leave or leave extensions are required?

Ans: American Red Cross

Where would a Navy family go to obtain an information packet containing materials on housing, commissaries, schools, and recreational activities available at a new duty station?

Ans: Family Services Center

What Department of Defense office is available to military families at most bases to provide real estate rental listings?

Ans: Housing Referral Office

PO1 UNIT IV

DAMAGE CONTROL; CBR DEFENSE

What are the three basic objectives of shipboard damage control?

Ans: Prevention, Minimization, and Restoration

What is meant by "prevention" as it pertains to damage control?

Ans: To take all practical preliminary measures, such as maintaining watertight integrity, providing reserve buoyancy/stability, removing fire hazards, and maintaining/distributing proper emergency equipment before damage occurs.

What is meant by the term "Minimization" as it applies to damage control?

Ans: To minimize/localize all damage by taking measures to control flooding, preserve stability and buoyancy, combat fires, and providing first aid.

What is the meaning of the term "Restoration" in damage control?

Ans: To accomplish emergency repairs after damage occurs (supplying emergency power, regaining stability of the ship, replacing essential structures, and manning all essential equipment.

Who in each division makes the assignments to repair parties?

Ans: The division officer

What are the first two steps in handling an at-sea casualty?

Ans: (1) Put out fires, and (2) Control flooding

What are two major kinds of flooding that can occur aboard ship?

Ans: Solid and Partial

What are flooding boundaries?

Ans: The bulkheads and decks restricting the partially flooded area from the flooding boundary

What are two factors that make repairs on underwater holes in ships difficult to repair?

Ans: Water pressure and accessibility

Who directs the shipboard training program for repair party leaders and division damage control petty officers?

Ans: Damage control assistant (DCA)

When entering a compartment aboard ship, where would you find information relating to the types of damage control fittings located within that space?

Ans: Compartment check-off list (CCOL)

If a compartment has two entrances to the space, how many compartment check-off lists are required to be posted within?

Ans: Two (one marked "Duplicate")

Who must ensure that safety precautions and operating instructions are posted in division spaces?

Ans: Division damage control petty officer

What is the normal shipboard battle station of the Damage Control Assistant?

Ans: Damage Control Central (DCC)

In any shipboard organization, who is responsible for ensuring the crew is adequately trained and continually exercised in all damage control aspects?

Ans: Commanding officer

What officer is charged with the overall responsibility for repairs to the ship's hull?

Ans: Engineering officer

Who is responsible for the general supervision of all phases of damage control aboard ship?

Ans: Executive officer

Who must ensure that repair party equipment is kept in the proper state of stowage and maintenance?

Ans: Repair party leader

What member of the repair party is known as the primary investigator?

Ans: #1 OBA Man

What is the designation of the damage control intercom system providing 2-way communications between DC Central and the repair stations?

Ans: 4MC

When does the most important phase of damage control take place?

Ans: Before damage occurs

What are the three basic purposes of first aid?

Ans: (1) To save life, (2) Prevent further injury, and (3) Preserve resistance and vitality.

What is the next step in procedure if it is determined that the at-sea fire party cannot bring a fire under control?

Ans: General quarters

What member of the repair party takes charge of all actions at the scene and directs the efforts of the repair party to fight fires, flooding, and structural damage?

Ans: Scene leader

What class of fire is a burning electrical motor?

Ans: C

What is the best extinguishing agent for an electrical fire?

Ans: CO2

What class of fire is burning gasoline?

Ans: B

Why are arrows painted on shipboard piping systems?

Ans: To distinguish the direction of flow

What shipboard condition of readiness provides maximum protection during battle?

Ans: ZEBRA

When can the effectiveness of damage control be properly tested?

Ans: When damage actually occurs

What publication contains a listing of available training courses, along with locations and prerequisites for formal damage control training?

Ans: Catalog of Naval Training Courses (CANTRAC)

How can you as a repair party leader ensure that the repair party will still be effective if one member of your team is injured?

Ans: Cross-train personnel in different tasks

The qualification of what standards ensures that personnel are knowledgeable of the ship's systems and damage control responsibilities?

Ans: Damage Control PQS

Once activated, how long will the emergency escape breathing device (EEBD) provide breathable air?

Ans: 15 minutes

What Navy command has the responsibility of forming doctrine and instructions for areas of damage control that are generally applicable to all ships?

Ans: Naval Sea Systems Command

What is the term used to describe any process which reduces or eliminates the effects of biological or chemical warfare agents at a particular point?

Ans: Decontamination

What would be the primary cause of injuries to topside personnel aboard a ship exposed to a nuclear air blast?

Ans: Bodily displacement

What is considered to be your personal first line of defense in the event of an CBR attack?

Ans: Protective mask

What is the proper action to take in reducing injuries caused by thermal radiation?

Ans: *Cover exposed skin surfaces and drop out of sight of the fireball*

Which of the nuclear radiation hazards will cause the least danger through contact with the skin?

Ans: *Alpha particles*

Because of their great penetrating power, which nuclear element presents the greatest danger to personnel?

Ans: *Neutrons*

What should a person do to reduce injuries when expecting an underwater shock?

Ans: *Hold on to solid structures, flex knees, and rest on the balls of your feet.*

What should be your very first action if there is any sign of a nerve agent in the atmosphere?

Ans: *Put on your protective mask*

What term describes the amount of biological or chemical agents actually absorbed by the body in a given period of time?

Ans: *Dose*

The hands-to-face method of evasion is designed to provide protection from what types of nuclear attack?

Ans: *Air blast & thermal radiation*

How should a liquid nerve agent be removed from the skin?

Ans: *Blotting with a cloth*

What is the best action to take if a nerve agent gets into your eye?

Ans: *Flush with uncontaminated water*

What is the antidote to be administered for nerve agents?

Ans: Atropine

When treating yourself with a nerve agent antidote, how many total injections may be given at ten minute intervals?

Ans: Three

What NBC agents have the odor of bitter almonds?

Ans: Blood agents

What chemical agents have physiological effects that are limited to the respiratory tract?

Ans: Choking agents

What treatment should be administered against blood agent poisoning?

Ans: Amyl nitrite

What is the purpose of radiological decontamination?

Ans: To remove contamination and shield personnel who must work in contaminated areas

What is the most practicable way to accomplish rapid decontamination of weather decks surfaces aboard ship?

Ans: Water washdown

What percentage of nuclear contamination can be removed from a ship's weather deck by the use of an effective water washdown system?

Ans: 85 percent

What NBC agents normally will not penetrate a painted surface?

Ans: Biological

What item of clothing should be removed last when a person is getting ready to enter the shower at a decontamination station?

Ans: Protective mask

Who is responsible for administering the shipboard CBR Defense Bill?

Ans: Damage Control Assistant (DCA)

What is the name of a flexible system of protection against chemical agents used in chemical warfare defense?

Ans: MOPP (Mission-Oriented Protective Posture)

How many levels of protection are designated within the MOPP?

Ans: Four

Facilities ashore must be prepared for disasters, (the restoration of mission-essential operations) by maintaining a disaster bill based on what instruction?

Ans: OPNAVINST 3120.32

What are the five phases of disaster relief operations?

Ans: (1) Planning, (2) Investigation of Extent of Disaster, (3) Initial Relief, (4) Routine Aid & Assistance, (5) Withdrawal

PO1 UNIT V

HUMAN RESOURCES MANAGEMENT

What is the purpose of the Navy's Human Resources Management Support System?

Ans: To promote the effective use of all the Navy's human potential

How does the Navy benefit by the use of Human Resources Management Support Systems to their full potential?

> *Ans: Improved combat readiness and capability*

What Navy program guarantees every sailor a fair chance for advancement and greater career satisfaction?

> *Ans: Equal Opportunity Program*

What Human Resources Management Support System program helps to promote satisfying overseas tours for naval personnel by conducting pre-deployment orientation briefings?

> *Ans: Overseas Duty Support Program*

What Navy program assists a Navy member and his family in getting settled in a new location through personal contact with other members of the new duty station?

> *Ans: Sponsor program*

What is the Navy's governing instruction concerning equal opportunity?

> *Ans: OPNAVINST 5354.1*

What type Navy commands must have and Equal Opportunity Program?

> *Ans: All commands*

To assure equal justice and treatment, how often should each command review charges, dismissals, warnings, and all NJP procedures?

> *Ans: Continually*

What type of action is a Navy member subject to if he/she intentionally takes residence in a facility which is under a military-imposed restrictive sanction?

> *Ans: Disciplinary action or loss of Basic Allowance for Quarters (BAQ)*

What amendment to the U.S. Constitution guarantees you to the rights of freedom of speech and assembly?

Ans: First

What is the task of the Command Assessment Team?

Ans: Evaluates how much command members actually know about equal opportunity

What is the task of the Command Training Team?

Ans: Assesses the command's compliance with the Navy's equal opportunity objectives as a whole

Name three methods of enforcing equal opportunity.

Ans: (1) Warning, (2) NJP, (3) Separation from the Navy

What are five counseling methods in order to instill in a subordinate the serious nature of the Navy's EO program?

Ans: (1) Verbal counseling, (2) Counseling through the use of locally prepared counseling sheets, (3) A letter of instruction (LOI), (4) A page 13 entry, and (5) A special evaluation.

What are some possible NJP mast punishments from Equal Opportunity violation?

Ans: (1) Restriction, (2) Correctional Custody, (3) Confinement on diminished rations, (4) Extra duty, (5) Forfeiture of pay, (6) Reduction in pay grade

Non-Judicial Punishment (NJP) is based on what article of the UCMJ?

Ans: Article 15

Prior to an NJP, on what form do you document a serious crime?

Ans: Report and Disposition of Offense(s), NAVPERS 1626/7

Normally, when does punishment take effect after an NJP?

Ans: Immediately

Can a service member appeal a punishment awarded at NJP?

Ans: Yes, within 5 days

Any supervisor who uses implicit or explicit sexual behavior to control, influence, or affect the career, pay, or job of any other person is guilty of what violation?

Ans: Sexual Harassment

From what two perspectives can equal opportunity be viewed?

Ans: (1) Personnel, and (2) Administrative

What is the Navy's goal concerning drug and alcohol abuse?

Ans: Zero tolerance

What are the two key elements for drug and alcohol abuse prevention?

Ans: Detection and deterrence

When is it consistent with Navy policy to introduce a narcotic or other controlled substance aboard a Navy ship?

Ans: When it is authorized for medical purposes

What command is responsible for drug and alcohol abuse education programs which are provided to Navy personnel?

Ans: Chief of Naval Education & Training (CNET)

What clue could indicate that a fellow sailor may be abusing or is possibly addicted to cocaine?

Ans: Red raw nostrils

The abuse of what type of drug may result in recurring effects weeks or months after the drug has been taken?

Ans: Hallucinogens

What are the effects of taking hallucinogenic drugs?

Ans: Distort the user's perceptions of objective reality

What type of drug is LSD?

Ans: Hallucinogen

What is the greatest danger to users of hallucinogens?

Ans: Unpredictability

Why does a marijuana abuser's mood and thinking change rapidly while smoking the substance?

Ans: The drug enters the bloodstream quickly.

What drugs will result in the user's appearance seeming similar to alcohol intoxication, except without the odor of alcohol on the breath?

Ans: Depressants

A drug abuser who constantly appears nervous and goes for long periods of time without sleep is a probable abuser of what type of drug?

Ans: Stimulants

What drug is often abused under the pretense of using them for weight control?

Ans: Amphetamines

What can be the result of using depressant drugs mixed with alcohol?

Ans: Unconsciousness and death

What Navy instruction states that drug and alcohol abuse is destructive to Navy personnel and will not be tolerated?

Ans: OPNAVINST 5350.4

Normally, what are the first emotional reactions following a dose of heroin?

Ans: An easing of fears followed by a state of stupor

A person who constantly drinks large amounts of cough syrup may possibly be an abuser of what type of drug?

Ans: Codeine

Alcohol is classified as what type of drug?

Ans: Depressant

Why do most people drink alcohol?

Ans: To get feelings of pleasure and relief of tension

What activity provides local assistance to fleet and shore commands in the counseling of personnel involved with drugs and alcohol?

Ans: Counseling & Assistance Centers (CAAC)

Which Navy program provides for the early identification of problem drinkers and drug abusers, and is designed to increase awareness of alcohol and drug abuse?

Ans: Navy Alcohol and Drug Safety Action Program (NADSAP)

Where in the human body does alcohol have its primary effect?

Ans: Central nervous system of the brain

What is likely to occur when a person has 0.40 percent or 0.50 percent alcohol in the blood?

Ans: Unconsciousness or coma

Why does alcohol affect the central nervous system so quickly?

> **Ans: It is immediately absorbed into the blood stream**

TRUE OR FALSE
In the chronic stages of alcoholism, a person's tolerance decreases to the point where he/she may become drunk on a very small amount of alcohol.

> **Ans: True**

What type of philosophy has the Navy adopted concerning the treatment of alcoholism?

> **Ans: It is a treatable disease**

What type of test is used by most states to determine whether or not a person is intoxicated?

> **Ans: Blood-alcohol level test**

What is the Navy's definition of alcoholism?

> **Ans: Psychological and/or physiological reliance on alcohol resulting from use on a periodic or continuing basis**

What is a common stigma about alcoholism that causes many problem drinkers to hide their problem rather than seek treatment?

> **Ans: That alcoholism is a moral weakness rather than a disease**

"The use of alcohol to an extent that it has an adverse effect on the user's health or behavior, family, community, or the Navy, or leads to unacceptable behavior as evidenced by an alcohol-related incident" is the Navy's definition of

> **Ans: alcohol abuse**

What person is the contact point for commanding officers seeking assistance or information on matters regarding drug and alcohol abuse?

Ans: Drug and Alcohol Abuse Counselor

Where are Alcohol Rehabilitation Services (ARS) offices located?

Ans: At Navy hospitals

What Navy program is designed to increase awareness of and build skills in the job competencies required for the effective performance of duties of officers and petty officers?

Ans: Leadership and Management Education and Training

The Navy has developed leadership & management training for personnel in what pay grades?

Ans: E-5 through 0-6

What term describes the knowledge, skills, and behaviors taught in Navy LMET courses to be used by superior leaders?

Ans: Competencies

What is the "government" system found aboard Navy ships?

Ans: Chain of command

"The art of influencing people to progress toward the accomplishment of a specific goal" is the Navy's definition of

Ans: leadership.

What is the most important factor to consider in leadership?

Ans: People

What should be one of your primary considerations concerning people when making decisions that affect a group?

Ans: Individual differences

What type of leadership are you using when you set the same standards for yourself that you expect from others?
Ans: Leadership by example

TRUE OR FALSE
Leadership and follower ship are opposites.
Ans: False

What is the basic purpose of all communicating?
Ans: Understanding

What trait of leadership is exhibited by a leader who makes decisions, good or bad, and accepts the responsibility and consequences for those decisions?
Ans: Accountability

Name two characteristics of goals set by effective leaders?
Ans: Realistic and challenging

What leadership skill includes breaking a job down into parts and determining specific steps to complete it?
Ans: Planning and organizing

What leadership and management category includes doing the right job at the right time in the correct manner?
Ans: Concern for efficiency and effectiveness

What leadership and management skill is used when a leader uses personnel available as fully as possible while assigning them meaningful work?

Ans: Optimizing use of resources

What leadership skill involves starting new plans or actions without being told to do so, and being resourceful in completing tasks as assigned?

Ans: Initiative

What is the purpose of a reprimand?

Ans: To teach

MILITARY REQUIREMENTS FOR CHIEF PETTY OFFICER

NOTE: While preparing for Chief Petty Officer, remember that you are also responsible for the standards and information at all lower levels. Review all previous material in this guide to enhance your readiness for the Military Requirements portion of Chief Petty Officer Exams.

CPO UNIT I

TRADITION & HISTORY

With what event did the naval affairs of the United States begin?

Ans: With the war for independence

When did Congress first approve legislation to purchase and arm two ships?

Ans: October 13, 1775

What are the 3 reasons for navy deployment of ships?

Ans: (1) Forces can engage the enemy promptly at the start of hostilities, (2) They can provide protection and support to allied forces, and (3) the can stop the advance of the enemy as soon as possible.

In a wartime posture, what is the two areas of responsibility of the Navy?

Ans: Sea control and power projection

How do most of the supplies supporting land warfare arrive on scene?

Ans: By sea

How does the U.S. maintain sea control?

Ans: By destroying or neutralizing hostile forces in maritime areas that we must use.

What is sea control?

Ans: The control of designated air, surface, and subsurface areas.

What is power projection?

Ans: The ability to project military power from the sea worldwide in a timely and precise manner to accomplish a given objective. Naval power projection is a means of supporting land or air campaigns.

What advantage of our Navy permits the concentration of naval forces and the element of surprise?

Ans: Mobility

What areas are the principal sources of oil for the industrial countries?

Ans: The Middle East and Southwest Asia

What "Choke Points" could be used to disrupt international shipping between the Mediterranean Sea and Indian Ocean, or between the rich oil countries and the rest of the world?

Ans: The Strait of Gibraltar and the Suez Canal

What region has 55 percent of the world's known oil reserves?

Ans: The Persian Gulf region

What was our goal in Operation Desert Shield and Desert Storm?

Ans: To deter Iraq from attacking Saudi Arabia and to convince Iraq to withdraw from Kuwait

Which United States fleet maintains a presence in the Middle East and Southwest Asia areas?

> ***Ans: Sixth Fleet in the Mediterranean, Sixth & Seventh Fleet in the Indian Ocean and Persian Gulf***

What is the purpose of our routine standing force in the Mediterranean?

> ***Ans: To ensure international waterways remain open to shipping in the region and provide forward deployed forces during hostilities***

Why is Northern Africa important from a naval viewpoint?

> ***Ans: Because it borders the Mediterranean Sea and the Red Sea.***

What is so important about Southern Africa from our naval viewpoint?

> ***Ans: Because of the vast wealth that it exports to developed countries***

What is the main and secondary mission of our Navy in the North African region?

> ***Ans: Main mission is to keep sea lanes open. Secondary mission is to support interest and political goals in that region.***

What is the main reason why we have nuclear ballistic missile submarines deployed?

> ***Ans: To deter war***

What is the mission of the RH-53D Stallion helicopter?

> ***Ans: Airborne mine countermeasures (AMCM)***

What is the mission of our A-6E Intruder aircraft?

> ***Ans: Strike & Recon***

What is the mission of the EA-6B Prowler aircraft?

> **Ans: EW & Recon**

What is the mission of the F-14 Tomcat?

> **Ans: Fleet long-range air defense**

What is the mission of the S-3A Viking?

> **Ans: ASW**

What is the mission of the F/A-18 Hornet?

> **Ans: Strike aircraft**

The mission of the P-3 Orion aircraft is

> **Ans: ASW**

Define the following terms as related to positions within a military formation:

> **Ans: ELEMENT: An individual, squad, section, platoon, company, or other unit that is part of a larger unit.**
>
> **FORMATION: An arrangement of elements in line, column, or in any other prescribed order.**
>
> **RANK or LINE: A formation of elements or persons abreast or side-by-side.**
>
> **FILE or COLUMN: A formation of elements or persons placed one behind the other.**
>
> **FLANK: The extreme right or left of a unit, either in line or in column. The element on the extreme right or left of the rank. A direction at a right angle to the direction an element or a formation is facing.**
>
> **DISTANCE: Within ranks, the space between the chest of one person and the back of the person ahead. Distance between ranks is 40 inches.**

INTERVAL: Normally, one arm's length measured between individuals from shoulder to shoulder.

GUIDE: The individual on whom a formation or element regulates its alignment. The guide is usually positioned to the right.

PACE: The length of a full step (30 inches for men, 24 inches for women)

STEP: The distance from heel to heel between the feet of a marching person. The half step and back step are 15 inches. The right and left steps are 12 inches.

The audit board that is responsible for auditing the chief petty officers' mess is composed of how many members?

Ans: Three

How often should the audit be conducted?

Ans: Monthly

What is the governing document concerning audit boards?

Ans: U.S. Navy Regulations

In what year did General Order 409 and U.S. Navy Regulation Circular #1 first list the Chief Petty Officer as a rate?

Ans: 1893

How many rows of medals would you have to wear if you rated six medals?

Ans: Two rows

How many rows of medals would wear if you rated 5 medals?

Ans: One row

CPO UNIT II

PUBLICATIONS, CORRESPONDENCE, & MANAGEMENT

What publication contains standards for the retention of naval records?

> *Ans: SECNAVINST 5212.5 (Disposal of Navy and Marine Corps Records)*

When does each fiscal year end?

> *Ans: 30 September*

What type of correspondence filing system exists when all originals of incoming & official copies of outgoing correspondence are filed in one specific office?

> *Ans: Centralized system*

What type correspondence filing system exists if the original or official copies are filed in the office or work center that has primary concern over the subject matter of the correspondence?

> *Ans: Decentralized system*

What publication outlines the organizational structure of the Department of the Navy, including principles and policies by which the Navy is governed?

> *Ans: United States Navy Regulations*

Who issues and approves changes to the United States Navy Regulations?

> *Ans: Issued by SECNAV, approved by the President*

What Naval Warfare publication lists and briefly describes all tactical warfare publications, including a discussion on the Naval Warfare Publications Library (NWPL)?

> *Ans: NWP 0 (Tactical Warfare Publications Guide)*

What types of tactical warfare publication discuss NATO operations, and often supplement information in Naval Warfare Publications (NWPs)?

Ans: Allied Tactical Publications (ATPs)

Who publishes Navy Ships Technical Manuals?

Ans: Naval Sea Systems Command

What types of publications contain instructions covering all phases of Navy communications?

Ans: Naval Telecommunications Publications (NTPs)

What publication contains policy, rules, and practices for administration of military personnel within the Navy?

Ans: Bureau of Naval Personnel Manual (BUPERSMAN)

What manual provides official information concerning the distribution and assignment of enlisted personnel of the U.S. Navy, and acts as a supplement to the MILPERSMAN?

Ans: Enlisted Transfer Manual (TRANSMAN)

What manual provides instructions for determining eligibility requirements for advancement, plus ordering, custody, disposition, and administration of Navy-wide examinations?

Ans: The Manual for Advancement

What type of communications publications outline procedures for communicating during NATO operations?

Ans: Allied Communications Publications (ACPs)

What type of communications publication is jointly issued by the Army, Navy, and Air Force discussing communications principles on jointly operated networks?

Ans: Joint Army-Navy-Air Force Publication (JANAP)

TRUE OR FALSE
The assignment of a Naval Warfare Publications Custodian is usually a collateral duty.

Ans: True

What periodical contains authoritative information on field changes, installation techniques, maintenance, beneficial suggestions, and distribution of technical manuals covering equipment such as communications, data systems, sonar, radar, and navigation?

Ans: Electronic Information Bulletin (EIB)

What publication is the Navy's guide to the organization of a unit?

Ans: Standard Organization and Regulations of the U. S. Navy (OPNAVINST 3120.32)

What type of bill assigns personnel to stations or duties that pertain to routine overall administration of the ship?

Ans: Administrative bill

What type of ship's bill assigns personnel to evolutions such as special sea detail and landing party?

Ans: Operational bill

What type of ship's bill assigns personnel to duties in situations such as man overboard, collision, and CBR defense?

Ans: Emergency bill

What naval warfare publication is used as a reference in preparing a ship's battle organization manual?

Ans: NWIP 50-1

What ships are exempt from preparing a battle organization manual and battle bill?

Ans: Those that have had a Ship Manning Document (SMD) issued

What document would you look for to obtain a listing of personnel reporting aboard soon or departing on PCS in the near future?

Ans: Enlisted Distribution Verification Report (EDVR)

What publication would provide you with format requirements when preparing a naval letter?

Ans: Department of the Navy Correspondence Manual (SECNAVINST 5216.5)

What is the first thing you should do when assigned a writing task?

Ans: Determine the deadline or target date for the correspondence

TRUE OR FALSE
Correspondence and documents should be classified according to their content and not necessarily according to their relationship to other documents.

Ans: True

Where can you find regulations and guidance for handling Equal Opportunity questions in the Navy?

Ans: OPNAVINST 5354.1

TRUE OR FALSE
References shown in the heading of a letter should be mentioned (in chronological order) within the text at least once.

Ans: True

TRUE OR FALSE
If space permits, an endorsement should be placed on the signature page of the basic letter.

Ans: True

What type of message has a wide standard distribution to all commands in an area under one command, or to types of commands and activities, such as "ALNAV," or "ALCOMPAC?"

Ans: General message

TRUE OR FALSE
General messages are numbered serially through the calendar year.

Ans: True

Who is responsible for the proper application of security classification and declassification markings during the composition of a message?

Ans: The drafter

Who is responsible for validating the contents of a message and affirming that the message is in compliance with message drafting instructions prior to transmission?

Ans: The releaser

Who is responsible for the proper addressing of an outgoing message?

Ans: The drafter

Who is responsible for selecting the appropriate precedence assigned to an outgoing message?

Ans: The drafter

What does the "precedence" of a message indicate to the telecommunications center?

Ans: The relative order of processing and delivery

What Naval Telecommunications Publication provides complete information concerning the assignment of message precedences?

Ans: NTP 3 (Telecommunications Users Manual)

What is the time standard for handling messages with "immediate" precedence assigned?

Ans: 30 minutes

What is the time standard for handling messages with "priority" precedence assigned?

Ans: 3 hours

What publication contains basic instructions concerning the format and procedures of a naval message?

Ans: NTP 3 Telecommunications Users Manual

What term denotes the format and ordinary language spelling of a command's short title and its geographical location used in naval messages?

Ans: Plain Language Address (PLA)

When used in naval telecommunications, what does the term "minimize" mean?

Ans: A condition imposed by proper authority to reduce and control electrical message and telephone traffic

What publication contains a listing of authorized standard subject identification codes (SSICs) to use when classifying naval documents by subject?

Ans: SECNAVINST 5210.11 (Department of the Navy Standard Subject Identification Codes)

In what line of a naval message is the standard subject identification code (SSIC) located?

Ans: At the end of the classification line

Under normal conditions, and unless otherwise directed, all message directives are automatically canceled how many days after the release date?

Ans: 90 days

What type of report conveys essentially the same type of information at regularly prescribed intervals?

> **Ans: Periodic report**

What type of report is prepared upon the occurrence of an event, such as an accident?

> **Ans: Situation report**

In order to be effective, how often should a tickler file be checked?

> **Ans: Daily**

What date is the end of the Navy's "Budget Year?"

> **Ans: 30 September**

How is money allocated to the Navy for spending?

> **Ans: Through an appropriations bill in Congress**

What is the objective of counseling shipmates?

> **Ans: To give your personnel support in dealing with problems so that they will regain the ability to work effectively in the organization.**

CPO UNIT III

PROFESSIONAL DEVELOPMENT AND ADMINISTRATION

The final multiple score on an examination is credit given for what three areas?

> **Ans: Performance, knowledge, & seniority**

What is the determining factor for the number of advancements authorized during each exam cycle?

> **Ans: Vacancies**

What is the current number of personnel on board a command versus the CNO requirements for a rating called?

Ans: Current inventory

Who establishes the maximum quota for each rating and gives the number of selection possibilities to each selection board panel?

Ans: Chief of Naval Personnel

What is the total active federal military service (TAFMS) requirement for E-7?

Ans: 11 years

Who establishes the requirements for total active federal military service (TAFMS)?

Ans: Department of Defense

What is the total percentage of personnel allowed to serve in pay grades E-7/8/9 that do not have the required TAFMS?

Ans: 10 percent

What is the pay grade of the individual who serves as the president of the CPO selection board?

Ans: Captain (0-6)

What is the single most important factor influencing whether or not an individual is selected for promotion to chief petty officer?

Ans: Sustained superior performance

What type of general message announces the selectees to CPO each year?

Ans: NAVADMIN

TRUE OR FALSE
If a person does not meet the Navy's weight standards when selected by the CPO board, advancement should be withheld until current standards are met.

Ans: *True*

TRUE OR FALSE
Test scores mean nothing to the CPO selection board. After the candidate attains a high enough score to become board eligible, the exam grade means nothing.

Ans: *False*

When a CPO selection board panel is finished scoring all records, the candidates are arranged by their numerical score from top to bottom. What is this process called?

Ans: *Slating*

What is a term for the administrative authorization to wear the uniform with rating insignia of a higher pay grade without the increased pay and allowances?

Ans: *Frocking*

What can you personally do to increase the chances of all pertinent information such as your self-improvements, accomplishments, and initiatives being properly documented in your annual performance evaluation?

Ans: *Submit an accurate and complete Individual Input Form (NAVPERS 1616/21)*

How long prior to the date of a convening CPO board should a PO1 request a copy of his enlisted summary record to ensure it is up to date?

Ans: *At least six months prior*

When are official microform personnel records at BUPERS normally updated?

Ans: *At the end of each enlistment or upon reenlistment*

Where should each letter of commendation or letter of appreciation that you receive be documented?

Ans: In your evaluation

Your permanent microform record at BUPERS contains all evaluations beginning at what pay grade?

Ans: E-5

TRUE OR FALSE
Your personnel office is required to send copies of each letter of appreciation you receive to BUPERS for your permanent record.

Ans: False

If you found errors in the copy of your record from BUPERS, and you are selection board eligible, where should you send copies of a corrected service record package?

Ans: One to BUPERS, and one to the president of the respective selection board

What pay grade is considered to be the senior "technician" in each rating?

Ans: E-7

What is the objective of the Career Counseling/Retention Team Program?

Ans: To obtain, on a long term basis, the maximum number of highly qualified enlisted personnel

What officer in the chain of command acts as the retention team coordinator?

Ans: XO (or staff equivalent)

Who is responsible for training the retention team members and ensuring appropriate facilities are available for interviews?

Ans: XO

Who is responsible for coordinating the training of all departmental/divisional retention team members in counseling techniques?

Ans: Command career counselor

What type entry should be made in a person's service record designating him/her as a department/division career counselor?

Ans: Page 13 entry

TRUE OR FALSE
All chief petty officers are members of the retention team, even though not assigned in writing.

Ans: True

During what retention team interview would a young seaman expect help in filling out his Enlisted Duty Preference Form?

Ans: Incentive programs interview

Who should conduct the retention interview on a person that just checked aboard the command?

Ans: Command career counselor (with division/department career counselor present)

What retention team interview explains SBP, social security, and benefits of remaining on active duty beyond the initial Fleet Reserve eligibility date?

Ans: Seventeen Year Monitoring Interview

During what retention team interview would an individual have veteran's benefits and VGLI insurance explained to him?

Ans: Pre-retirement/Separation Interview

Name the six general rates that exist at the E-3 level.

Ans: Airman, Fireman, Seaman, Dentalman, Constructionman, Hospitalman

When were specialty marks added to the enlisted uniforms in order to distinguish between ratings?

Ans: 1866

What is the purpose of the Navy Enlisted Classification (NEC) structure?

Ans: To supplement the enlisted rating structure

On what page of your service record are NEC codes entered?

Ans: Page 4

What does the Navy Enlisted Classification (NEC) code represent?

Ans: Special knowledge and skills that are not rating-wide requirements

In what two ways do you become more valuable to the Navy as you are advanced?

Ans: As a specialist, and as an instructor

What is the minimum rate that an enlisted member must hold for eligibility prior to applying for warrant officer?

Ans: Chief petty officer (E-7)

How long must a Naval Academy graduate serve on active duty after graduation?

Ans: Five years

After you are discharged from active duty with no disability, your SGLI coverage will continue for a maximum of how many days?

Ans: 120 days

Who assigns the members of a special court martial to try a member aboard a ship?

Ans: Commanding officer

"Reaching goals through the effective use of personnel and other resources" is a partial description of

> ### Ans: management.

What are the functions of management?

> ### Ans: Planning, organizing, directing (supervising), and controlling

What function of management includes recognizing the need for action, setting objectives, investigating and analyzing the situation, determining courses of action, and making decisions?

> ### Ans: Planning

What term describes the power to make a decision and to command others to act?

> ### Ans: Authority

Why should supervisors consider at least two courses of action when planning?

> ### Ans: It will allow all facets of the problem to be considered

How far down the chain of command should authority be delegated?

> ### Ans: Down to the lowest competent level

What term within Leadership & Management training describes any knowledge, skill, behavior, or thought pattern that distinguishes between effective and less effective job performance?

> ### Ans: Competency

What document is used to determine if an individual is eligible for reenlistment, honorable discharge, or a Good Conduct Medal?

> ### Ans: Performance evaluation

Navy personnel in pay grades E-6 and below do not receive an evaluation grade in what area?

Ans: Management

TRUE OR FALSE
An evaluation must be submitted any time a person is permanently transferred from one command to another.

Ans: True

As a minimum, how often must evaluations be submitted on each enlisted member?

Ans: Annually

Guidelines for submitting enlisted evaluations are found in what publication?

Ans: Naval Military Personnel Manual

Who are individuals graded against on their evaluations?

Ans: Personnel in the same pay grade

When constructing a test, what is a complete question called?

Ans: An "item"

What are the incorrect responses supplied with multiple-choice questions called?

Ans: Distracters

On a written test, the part of a question that provides the statement or situation which is to be completed or analyzed is called

Ans: the stem.

What types of test questions allow the student to select the correct answer from a list of alternatives?

Ans: Objective (or "selection") type

What type of test questions call for the student to supply the answer in the form of essay, short answer, or by completion?

Ans: Subjective (or "supply") type

What types of test questions are best suited to test knowledge of technical terms?

Ans: Objective ("selection") type

What types of test questions are best for testing a person's self-expression ability?

Ans: Essay (Subjective)

TRUE OR FALSE
When developing "true or false" questions for a test, you should try to avoid using such words as "all," "never," "always," and "sometimes."

Ans: True

When constructing a test, where is the suggested placement of the easiest questions?

Ans: Near the front of the test

What type of test question best evaluates the student's ability to form new ideas?

Ans: Essay (Subjective) type

What time of day is best suited for administering tests?

Ans: Morning

At what point in their career should a person have his/her first career counseling session?

Ans: About 2 years into their career

How are weight allowances for household goods determined?

Ans: By a person's paygrade

What is the dislocation allowance based on?

> *Ans: DLA is equal to 1 month's basic allowance for quarters (BAQ) for your dependency status and paygrade.*

What is the job of the Command Master Chief?

> *Ans: He/she serves as the senior enlisted adviser in setting command policy about morale, use and training of all enlisted personnel. The C/MC has direct access to the CO.*

Who normally sits as members of the Chief Petty Officer's Selection Board?

> *Ans: A captain as president, a junior officer as recorder, and officers and master chief petty officers serving as board/panel members. Additional E-7, E-8 and E-9's can serve as additional recorders to ensure a smooth handling of records.*

Who may be transferred to the Fleet Reserve?

> *Ans: Any member upon completion of at least 20 years active service in the armed forces.*

Who gets transferred to the Regular Navy Retired List?

> *Ans: Any member who has completed 30 years service (including Active Duty and Fleet Reserve time, if any).*

What documents should be included in the short-range training plan?

> *Ans: The Quarterly Employment Schedule, The Quarterly Training Plan, The Monthly Training Plan, and the Weekly Training Schedule.*

What are the three basic features of an effective training program?

> *Ans: Compatibility, Evaluation & Instruction, and Analysis & Improvement*

What is meant by the term "compatibility" when referring to a training program?

> Ans: *The training program must work with the command framework and schedule*

What is meant by the term "Instruction" in a training program?

> Ans: *The actual training of personnel*

What is meant by the term "Analysis" concerning a training program?

> Ans: *Observing group or individual performance and comparing the results with standard criteria.*

What type of training are drills and exercises conducted in port or underway?

> Ans: *Team Training*

CPO UNIT IV

HUMAN RESOURCES MANAGEMENT AND SAFETY

In what three areas does the Human Resources Management Center (HRMC) assist commanding officers?

> Ans: *(1) Sustaining combat readiness, (2) Achieving mission accomplishment, and (3) Retaining qualified personnel*

What Navy instruction outlines the Navy's policy concerning Equal Opportunity?

> Ans: *OPNAVINST 5354.1*

What is the name of the written document at each Navy command that outlines specific problems and proposes solutions toward achieving equal opportunity?

> **Ans: Affirmative Action Plan (AAP)**

TRUE OR FALSE
The contents of the Affirmative Action Plan (AAP) is the same at all commands.

> **Ans: False**

TRUE OF FALSE
The Affirmative Action Plan (AAP) should be well-publicized and be available to everyone in the command.

> **Ans: True**

What instruction outlines procedures for discrimination complaints?

> **Ans: OPNAVINST 5354.1**

Who in the Navy may file a complaint of oppression, misconduct, or disparate treatment against a supervisor?

> **Ans: Any person**

When a discrimination complaint cannot be immediately resolved with the help of the supervisor, what is the first course of action the supervisor should take?

> **Ans: Advise the complainant to submit a special request chit to the chain of command**

When a JAG Manual informal investigation is ordered, the appointed investigator should be of what minimum rank/rate?

> **Ans: At least a chief petty officer**

What levels of the Navy leadership should have thorough knowledge of the current drug problem?

> **Ans: All levels**

TRUE OR FALSE
Retired military personnel and their dependents do NOT receive assistance from Family Service Centers.

Ans: False

TRUE OR FALSE
One goal of the Overseas Duty Support Program (ODSP) is to increase individual leave/liberty satisfaction.

Ans: True

TRUE OR FALSE
A chief petty officer who is caught using illicit drugs will normally be given a second chance to complete his career.

Ans: False

What is the Navy's goal concerning drug and alcohol abuse?

Ans: Zero tolerance

What instruction contains the basic policy guidance regarding the Navy's Alcohol and Drug Abuse Control Program?

Ans: SECNAVINST 5300.28

What Navy program is designed to increase the Navy's awareness of and access to useful, reliable information, resources, and services that enrich the lives of Navy families and single service members?

Ans: Family Support Program

An amphetamine user is usually characterized by excessive activity. What type of drugs are amphetamines?

Ans: Stimulants

Barbiturates are classified as what type of drug?

Ans: Depressant

What would be characteristic about the nose of an individual who has inhaled large quantities of heroin or cocaine?

Ans: Red and raw nostrils

If you overheard a person discussing illegal drugs, the term "reefer" would be in reference to what kind of drug?

Ans: Marijuana cigarette

The odor of marijuana burning is similar to

Ans: Burnt rope

What type drug is LSD?

Ans: Hallucinogen

TRUE OR FALSE
The effects of LSD may recur days or months after the drug has been taken.

Ans: True

TRUE OR FALSE
Alcohol is classified as a drug.

Ans: True

What are the largest treatment facilities in the Navy's alcoholism treatment and rehabilitation program called?

Ans: Alcohol Rehabilitation Centers (ARCs)

A burn that destroys the skin and possibly the tissue and muscle beneath it is classified as what degree of burn?

Ans: Third degree

A burn that produces blisters, severe pain, some dehydration, and possible shock is classified as what degree of burn?

Ans: Second degree

A burn that produces redness in skin, tenderness and slight pain is classified as what degree of burn?

Ans: First degree

How much blood loss will usually cause a person to go into shock?

Ans: 2 pints

In almost all cases, bleeding can be stopped by what method?

Ans: Application of direct pressure on the wound

According to Navy industrial safety records, how many minor injuries occur for every severe injury?

Ans: 25 to 30

What class of mishap is one that the resulting total cost of property damage and personnel injuries is $500,000 or more, or an injury/illness results in a fatality or permanent total disability?

Ans: Class A Mishap

What class of mishap has occurred if the total cost of property damage and personnel injuries is between $100,000 and $500,000, or an injury/illness results in permanent partial disability or the hospitalization of 5 or more personnel?

Ans: Class B Mishap

What class of mishap is one that results in the total cost of property damage and personnel injuries of between $10,000 and $100,000, or an injury/illness results in a lost work day case with days away from work?

Ans: Class C Mishap

TRUE OR FALSE
People cause mishaps. Therefore, prevention actions must be directed at people.

Ans: True

What class of mishap results in the total cost of property damage and personnel injuries is less than $10,000, or an injury results in a lost workday case with days of restricted work activity; or a nonfatal case without lost workdays?

Ans: Class D Mishap

What percentage of all mishaps is caused by unsafe conditions?

Ans: 10 percent

What percentage of all mishaps is caused by unsafe acts?

Ans: 85 percent

Unrealistic confidence is an effect of what medical cause factor of mishaps?

Ans: Alcohol consumption

What term refers to the mixing of two or more drugs?

Ans: Polydrugs

For what purpose is the information gained from a mishap investigation used?

Ans: To develop preventive measures

Extreme exposure to heat, cold, vibration, noise, illumination, radiation, or atmospheric contaminants are examples of what factors contributing to mishaps?

Ans: Environmental factors

TRUE OR FALSE
Any mishap, near mishap, or situation that could result in a mishap should be investigated and subsequently reported.

Ans: True

What Navy instruction will assist a person conducting a mishap investigation to prepare a complete and meaningful report?

> *Ans: OPNAVINST 5102.1 (Mishap Investigation and Reporting)*

What Navy instruction provides guidance concerning privacy act statements required in investigations?

> *Ans: SECNAVINST 5211.5 (Privacy Act)*

What type of questions should NOT be asked during the early stages of a mishap investigation interview?

> *Ans: "Why" questions*

What should be the minimum basic elements in a safety program?

> *Ans: (1) Safety standards/regulations, (2) Mishap prevention education & training, (3) Maintenance, (4) Safety enforcement, & (5) Mishap investigating/reporting.*

What is a major function of the Family Service Center (FSC)?

> *Ans: to prevent problems and to enhance family life*

What program offers support to a next of kin of Navy members involved in a casualty?

> *Ans: The Casualty Assistance Calls Program (CACP)*

What instruction provides guidance for all commands and units in taking part in the Navy Sponsor Program?

> *Ans: OPNAVINST 1740.3*

What Navy program helps personnel and their families deal with various overseas cultures?

> *Ans: The Overseas Duty Support Program (ODSP)*

What trait of "Pride and Professionalism" is being displayed when you are dedicated to your job?

Ans: Devotion to duty

What trait of "Pride and Professionalism" is being displayed when you are faithful to your commitments or obligations?

Ans: Loyalty

When making a report of an offense, what are the qualities that should always exist?

Ans: Who, What, Where, When, and How

Where should you begin to look for bargains in recreation, recreation equipment, and recreation facilities?

Ans: Your Morale, Welfare, and Recreation (MWR) Department

CPO UNIT V

MATERIAL MANAGEMENT

If you wish to trace one of your supply requisitions, what organizational component of the shore supply department would you contact?

Ans: Issue Control Branch

What organizational component of a shore supply department monitors and expedites material due or arriving from outside sources?

Ans: Receipt Control Branch

What division of the shore supply department maintains warehouses, storerooms, and receives, stores, and issues materials?

Ans: Material Division

What division is normally the stores division aboard ship?

Ans: S-1 Division

TRUE OR FALSE
Storage of ammunition aboard ship is not under the control of the supply department.

Ans: True

Administrative and housekeeping items, general purpose hardware, common tools, and other items not specifically defined as equipment, equipage, or repair parts are classified as what category of material?

Ans: Consumables

What officer exercises control over the overall ship's equipage allowance?

Ans: Supply officer

What is the term described by the period of time required for a ship to use a definite quantity of supplies?

Ans: Endurance

What is the most accurate guide in the determination of a ship's material requirements?

Ans: The ship's experience as shown in accurate stock records

Who heads the supply department on small ships where there is no supply corps officer assigned?

Ans: A line officer

What two factors determine what available priority is assigned to each requisition?

Ans: The military importance of the activity and the urgency of the requirement

Who has the responsibility for assigning the proper priority designator to a requisition for repair parts?

Ans: Commanding officer

What officer or department assigns the appropriate "urgency of need" code to a material request?

Ans: The customer department

What are the two most common documents used to request and issue material?

Ans: NAVSUP Form 1250 and DD Form 1348

When stowing material aboard ship, what is placed under the material to keep it from direct contact with the dampness of the deck?

Ans: Dunnage

TRUE OR FALSE
Supply items should be stowed so that the newest items received onboard are used first.

Ans: False

TRUE OR FALSE
In almost all cases, material should NOT be stowed in stock number sequence, because national stock numbers assigned are not necessarily related to item characteristics.

Ans: True

What is the term applied to selected items of equipage which require increased management control afloat because of high unit cost, vulnerability to pilferage, or that are essential to ship's mission?

Ans: Controlled equipage

TRUE OR FALSE

The commanding officer may change controlled equipage "nonsignature - required" items to "signature - required" items when he considers such additional control necessary.

> ### Ans: True

What is the prescribed form for use as a custody record and inventory control document for controlled equipage items in non-automated ships?

> ### Ans: Controlled Equipage Custody Record (NAVSUP Form 306)

What is used as the department's basic custody record for controlled equipage items?

> ### Ans: The duplicate copy of NAVSUP Form 306

Who maintains the original copy of all controlled equipage custody records?

> ### Ans: Supply officer

A survey is required whenever Navy property is lost, damaged, or destroyed. What is the purpose of a survey?

> ### Ans: To determine the responsibility for lost, damaged, or destroyed property and to fix the actual loss to the government

What survey form must be prepared when personal responsibility for loss, damage, or destruction of property is NOT evident?

> ### Ans: DD Form 2090

What survey form must be prepared if personal responsibility for lost, damaged, or destroyed property is evident?

> ### Ans: DD Form 200

How often are all items of controlled equipage inventoried?

> ### Ans: Annually between 15 Feb - 15 Mar

There are always many stores in the technical custody of the supply department but in the physical custody of other departments. When are these items inventoried?

Ans: At the end of each quarter, or when prescribed by the supply officer

What is the determining factor of why material is designated under selected item management (SIM) or Non-SIM?

Ans: Frequency of demand

What type team assists a ship's supply officer in planning, preparing, and completing a supply overhaul during the ship's regularly scheduled overhaul?

Ans: Integrated Logistics Overhaul (ILO) Team

A complete verification of all installed electronic equipments (less fire control) can be completed by comparing what document with a list of onboard equipment?

Ans: Ship Equipment Configuration Accounting System (SECAS) Inventory Report

Why are operating target (OPTAR) funds divided into departmental budgets?

Ans: To promote cost consciousness and to equitably distribute funds

CPO UNIT VI

CBR DEFENSE EQUIPMENT

Who coordinates the relieving, qualifying, training, and duties of the divisional damage control petty officers as directed by the ship's DCA and fire marshall?

Ans: Departmental Damage Control Chief Petty Officer

Using the Navy's system of classifying BW/CW protective clothing, what is the class of impregnated clothing?

Ans: Z

In the Navy's system of classifying BW/CW protective clothing, what is the designated class of wet weather clothing?

Ans: X

What is the designated class of BW/CW protective clothing when wet-weather gear is worn over the top of impregnated clothing?

Ans: XZ

As a minimum, how often should a ship's impregnated clothing be checked to determine the activity of the CC2 impregnate?

Ans: Annually

TRUE OR FALSE
Exposure to sunlight decreases the effectiveness of protective impregnated clothing.

Ans: True

Why is it necessary to wear wet-weather clothing as an outside garment over impregnated clothing when going topside as a protective measure against CW agents?

Ans: Large aerosol particles or droplets may penetrate the fabric of impregnated clothing in strong winds.

What is the principal deterioration factor of the neutralizing chemical CC2 in impregnated clothing?

Ans: Moisture

Why is the tolerance level limited when using wet-weather clothing?

Ans: No air can pass through the clothing to assist in cooling the wearer's body

What fittings should be closed aboard ship to prevent chemical or biological agents from entering the ship's ventilation system?

Ans: CIRCLE WILLIAM

What is the unit of measurement when discussing the exposure dose of radiation?

Ans: Roentgen (R)

What is the unit of measurement when discussing the absorbed dose of radiation?

Ans: Rads

What device measures the total radiation received by an individual exposed to radiation?

Ans: Dosimeter

What two types of dosimeters are in use in the Navy?

Ans: Self-reading and nonself-reading

Excessive flow of saliva, intestinal cramps, nausea, vomiting, and diarrhea are all symptoms that you may have swallowed what king of poisonous vapors?

Ans: Nerve agent

What nerve agent antidote is contained in personal decontamination kits?

Ans: Atropine

When decontaminating a weather deck using a fire hose, how far from the hose nozzle should the water strike the deck?

Ans: 8 feet

How many personnel normally make up a radiation-monitoring team?

Ans: Three

What areas are most important when a radiation-monitoring team is taking readings?

Ans: The areas that will be occupied by people

On what type of readings does a radiation-monitoring team depend to identify areas most in need of decontamination?

Ans: Gamma

How many protective masks are provided to each ship?

Ans: Equal to 105 percent of wartime personnel complement

You test a donned protective mask for leakage by inhaling while covering the canisters with the palms of your hand. How long should the mask remain collapsed against your face?

Ans: Approximately 10 seconds

TRUE OR FALSE
In CBR defense, the protective mask is the most important item of equipment, since it protects your eyes, face, and respiratory tract.

Ans: True

TRUE OR FALSE
The protective mask DOES NOT provide protection against gases such as carbon monoxide, carbon dioxide, tritium, and ammonia.
Ans: True

TRUE OR FALSE
The protective mask would be an ideal garment to wear for protection in spaces that have a deficiency of oxygen.

Ans: False

What type of protective mask is issued to shore-based personnel?

Ans: The M17-series mask

What two requirements must be met for a protective mask to accomplish purification of air?

Ans: The face piece must fit snugly over the face, and the filter system must function properly.

How many sizes are available in the M17 series protective masks?

Ans: Three (small, medium, & large)

How many sizes are available in the ND MK V protective mask?

Ans: One

When donning the M17 series protective mask, you must slip the mask over what portion of the face first?

Ans: The chin

How often should the M17 series protective mask be inspected during peacetime conditions?

Ans: Every 6 months

What are the only authorized items that should be placed in the ND MK V carrier along with the mask?

Ans: A protective ointment kit and antidim

What is the purpose of antidim being stowed in the carrier along with the ND MK V protective mask?

Ans: Reduces fogging of the mask eyepiece when applied to its interior

CPO UNIT VII

MILITARY JUSTICE, LEADERSHIP, & SECURITY

What are the duties of a Preliminary Inquiry Officer (PIO)?

Ans: Conduct an investigation of offenses before a captain's mast takes place

What should be your primary objective in conducting a preliminary inquiry?

Ans: To collect all available evidence pertaining to the alleged offense

What should be your secondary objective in conducting a preliminary inquiry?

Ans: Collect information about the accused (current duties, evaluation, attitudes, personal difficulties, etc.)

What is considered the BEST SOURCE of information about the accused?

Ans: Statements given by supervisors, peers, and the accused person

When during your investigation should you interrogate the accused?

Ans: Leave the accused to last

What should you become familiar with prior to seeking any real evidence?

Ans: Become familiar with Military Rules of Evidence concerning searches and seizures in the Manual for Courts-Martial.

Before questioning the accused, what should be your first order of business?

> **Ans: Have the accused sign the acknowledgment line on the front of report chit, correctly advising him/her of rights**

If the accused does not wish to write out a statement, what is desired?

> **Ans: A certified summary of the interrogation attached to the report**

What chapter of Navy Regulations describes the general authority and responsibilities of the commanding officer?

> **Ans: Chapter 8**

How often should Article 137 of UCMJ be explained to an individual while serving in the Navy?

> **Ans: (1) At the time of entrance to the Navy, (2) after six months active duty, and (3) upon each reenlistment**

TRUE OR FALSE
Members on the U.S. Navy Retired List with pay are at all times subject to naval authority.

> **Ans: TRUE**

Is it legal for a service member to communicate with a congressman?

> **Ans: Yes, they may write their congressman on any subject as long as they do not violate any security regulations or the law.**

What chapter of Navy Regulations covers Flags, Pennants, Honors & Customs?

> **Ans: Chapter 12**

How long is the normal assignment for EMI?

Ans: Normally, not longer than 2 hours per day

What happens to a person's personal effects after he/she has been declared a deserter?

Ans: They are collected, inventoried, and sealed by a division petty officer in the presence of the division officer and a master-at-arms and delivered to the CMAA for safekeeping and disposition.

Who publishes/issues the Plan of the Day?

Ans: The Executive Officer

Who signs the Plan of the Day if the XO is gone?

Ans: The Command Duty Officer

Agreements with several of our allied countries to protect the American's rights while serving overseas are known as

Ans: The Status of Forces Agreements (SOFAs)

What is the main purpose of the Status of Forces Agreements?

Ans: To clearly define the status of one country's military personnel stationed in the territory of another

What is the general United States feeling toward trying U.S. military personnel in foreign courts?

Ans: The U.S. government objects to it

In accordance with most Status of Forces Agreements, what is the U.S. government right if a U.S. military person is sentenced to confinement in a foreign prison?

Ans: American authorities are permitted frequent visits to check on well being of individual, also person is allowed to receive health-benefiting items, items of comfort, and food items considered necessary to an American's diet.

What is one significant advantage of a military member being tried in a foreign court over those facing trial in the U.S.?

Ans: Congress has authorized the armed services to pay attorney fees and court costs as well as provide for bail in appropriate cases

If you commit an offense on foreign soil, how can you be tried by the courts of your military service?

Ans: Only by the consent of the host country

Within the formal Navy management structure, where does "management" begin?

Ans: at the Chief Petty Officer level

Within the formal Navy management structure, what is "middle management" composed of?

Ans: Heads of Departments

"Operating-level management" is composed of

Ans: Division officers and chief petty officers

What are plans?

Ans: Methods devised to achieve a certain goal

"U.S. Navy Regulations" and "Standard Organization and Regulations of the U.S. Navy" are known as what kind of plan?

Ans: Standing plans

Define a policy

Ans: Broad general statements of expected behavior

What is a "procedure?"

Ans: A detailed standing plan, defining the exact steps in sequence that personnel should take to achieve the objective

What type of standing plan specifically states what personnel can and cannot do in a given circumstance?

Ans: Rules and Regulations

What type plans are used for short-range nonrecurring activities?

Ans: Single-Use plans

What type plans state a specific goal and give the major steps, the timing of the steps, and the resources required to achieve the goal?

Ans: A Program

What type of plan is planned revenue and expenditures of money, time, personnel, equipment, etc. expressed in numerical terms?

Ans: A budget

What type management is being used when supervisors and subordinates take part in setting overall goals for the organization?

Ans: Management by Objectives (MBO)

What is the purpose of "Management by Objectives?"

Ans: to set clearly defined goals that all participants can easily understand

What are the two basic principles of Management by Objectives?

Ans: (1) you get people committed to a goal, and (2) if you allow people to set the goals, they will do everything possible to achieve the goal

What are some disadvantages to "Management by Objectives?"

Ans: It requires more time to use, it increases paper work, and it may overlook objectives that cannot be measured. It also will only work if the top leaders support it. People must communicate.

What is feedforward control?

> *Ans: A way of trying to anticipate problems and make adjustments before the problems occur*

What is concurrent control?

> *Ans: Making changes while an event is taking place*

What is feedback?

> *Ans: Making corrections after an event has happened. You monitor the event and make changes to improve the outcome the next time.*

What three specific types of organization does the Navy employ?

> *Ans: Line, Staff, and Functional*

What is a Line Organization?

> *Ans: A major department responsible for accomplishing the mission of the command. Examples would be Deck, Engineering, Operations, Weapons, & Air departments aboard a ship.*

What is a Staff Organization?

> *Ans: Personnel who assist, counsel, and serve the line departments. Examples would be Supply, 3-M Coordinator, & ESO.*

What is a Functional Organization?

> *Ans: A special department that is neither staff nor line, such as Medical, Safety, Legal, and Admin.*

What is the definition of "Chain of Command?"

> *Ans: The order of authority among Navy members. At the local level, it begins with the CO, and works down to the lowest rated seaman recruit.*

What quality of an organization ensures that a person reports directly to and receives orders from only one individual?

> *Ans: Unity of Command*

What term refers to the "ideal number of people that one person can effectively supervise?"

> *Ans: Span of Control*

What term in the organization structure refers to the division of work?

> *Ans: Specialization*

Why should a supervisor delegate his authority?

> *Ans: Delegating allows you to accomplish more than if you tried to complete every task yourself.*

When speaking of Authority and Power, what is line authority?

> *Ans: The authority that you have over subordinates in your chain of command*

What is staff authority?

> *Ans: The right of staff personnel to counsel, advise, or make recommendations to line personnel*

What are some traits that may be exhibited by a "Coercer" style of leadership?

> *Ans: A "coercer" leader expects the job to be done exactly as the subordinates have been told. A coercer leader provides clear directions by telling the workers what to do and how to do it.*

What are some characteristics of an "Authoritarian" style of leadership?

Ans: Firm but fair leader. The authoritarian leader tactfully provides clear direction, but leaves no doubt about what is expected or who makes the final decisions. The leader may solicit some input from the subordinates on how to do the job. An authoritarian sees his/her influence as a major part of the job.

What style of leadership is exhibited if the leader's first concern is for his/her people?

Ans: An "Affiliator"

What style of leadership is displayed when success relies on participation in the decision-making from the group?

Ans: Democratic

What type of leadership style is shown when the leader would rather do the job himself?

Ans: Pacesetter

What type leaders see their job as developing and improving the performances of their subordinates, are concerned with high standards, but have trouble communicating these standards to subordinates?

Ans: Coach style of leadership

Name the five management and supervisory skills required to maintain an effective work center.

Ans: (1) Concern for Standards, (2) Concern for Efficiency, (3) Planning & Organizing, (4) Supervising for Effective Performance, and (5) Monitoring

What personal characteristic does a Chief display when seeking new challenges and working to reach higher levels of accomplishment?

Ans: Concern for Achievement

What personal characteristic would a Chief be exhibiting when analyzing a complex situation and evaluating information to choose the best solution to a problem?

Ans: Analytical Problem Solving

What personal characteristic is displayed when a CPO expends an extraordinary effort to complete a task?

Ans: Persistence

What personal characteristic is shown by the Chief who confronts issues directly and insists that others recognize his/her place in the chain of command?

Ans: Assertiveness

Who is responsible for setting up and maintaining an Information Security Program and a Personnel Security Program?

Ans: Secretary of the Navy

Who did the SECNAV make responsible for information and personnel security?

Ans: Chief of Naval Operations

What Navy instruction series contains the information on the Navy Personnel Security Program?

Ans: SECNAVINST 5510.30 Series

What organization provides the overall guidance on information and personnel security?

Ans: National Security Council (NSC)

What is the chief internal security agency of the federal government?

Ans: The FBI

Who at the local command is overall responsible for the effective management of the Department of the Navy Information and Personnel Security Program?

Ans: Commanding Officer

What are the normal rank requirements of the command security manager?

Ans: An officer or if a civilian, GS-11 or above

What is a "compromise" of classified information?

Ans: the disclosure of classified information to a person who is not authorized access to that information

What actions should be taken if you find a security container with classified documents stored inside open and unattended?

Ans: Report incident to duty officer, make sure container is guarded until duty officer arrives on scene.

What are the three security classification designations?

Ans: Confidential, Secret, & Top Secret

How long should records be kept showing the number of copies and distribution of a Top Secret document?

Ans: Two years

When should all classified documents be destroyed?

Ans: As soon as they are no longer required

What method of destruction of classified material is the most traditional and effective?

Ans: Burning

Because of the Clean Air Act, burning is not always possible. What is the next best way to destroy classified material?

Ans: Shredding machines

Prior to granting a Security Clearance, a person's loyalty, reliability, and trustworthiness is determined. How is this normally accomplished?

Ans: by the Personnel Security Investigation

Who grants access to classified information at the local command?

Ans: The Commanding Officer

ANNEX D

SELECTION BOARDS

Advancement opportunity in the Navy is unlimited, based on a person's willingness to work and study with diligence. Advancement to chief petty officer or an appointment to commissioned status is the normal goal of most enlisted personnel. Selection normally requires a clean service record, excellent professional performance, and some good examination scores. Also included in the selection prerequisites should be some careful career planning.

This section will first provide basic information about how a selection board conducts its business, plus give some insight on how to make yourself promotable (via your service record) before a selection board. The examples provided within this section will be for a CPO selection board, but all others are similarly conducted with minor variations.

HOW THE BOARD OPERATES

Each CPO selection board has a Navy Captain who serves as president of the board. A junior officer acts as recorder, plus several E-7/8/9 personnel are assigned as assistant recorders. 60 or more officers and senior/master chief petty officers may be assigned as board/panel members.

PRECEPTS

The selection board is appointed by the Chief of Naval Personnel. The Secretary of the Navy, CNO, NMPC, and the Enlisted Community Managers also make inputs to the board. A "precept" is prepared each year outlining guidance and general information on how to conduct the board. These precepts are normally general in nature, and can vary slightly from year to year. Precepts usually include such guidelines as:

- The board members should only compare candidates with other candidates in the same rating.

- The quotas established for each rating must not be exceeded.

- Each candidate must be fully qualified for advancement and be capable of performing required duties.

- Considerations should be given to continuing education.

- The board is provided instructions on where to find required information in the microform service record of each individual

- An overweight problem should not hinder an individual's selection potential. However, advancement will be withheld until standards are met.

- Advancement will not be denied solely on the basis of prior alcoholism or alcohol abuse provided the member has participated in successful treatment and recovery.

- Significant emphasis shall be given to sustained professional performance at sea, while recognizing that some ratings do not offer a broad opportunity for sea duty.

- Due consideration is given for those serving outside their rating, especially those who have had demanding tours as instructor, recruiter, career counselor, recruit company commander, etc.

- Marks and narrative must correspond on evaluations. Consideration is given for letters of commendation/appreciation, personal decorations, etc. Superior performance of duty remains most important.

GROUND RULES

The board establishes internal ground rules and minimum selection criteria for each board member to use when screening candidates' records. The application of these rules may vary slightly from one rating to another, for reasons such as difference in types of duty available in the rating, lack of available service schools, lack of supervisory opportunities, different rotation patterns, etc.

Selection boards may also be told to give "special emphasis" to certain areas of consideration. For example, CNO may direct the board to provide emphasis to personnel serving outside their rating in instructor billets, or to those personnel with a warfare qualification (EAWS, ESWS, etc.). If this occurs, the selection board will agree to provide proper emphasis in these areas.

POINT VALUES

Before the actual screening process begins, the board decides on the categories that will be receiving "points" toward selection. Categories such as evaluations, career history, duty assignments, etc., are determined along with the maximum number of points that may be awarded in each area. Boards vary in the "amount" of total points. Some work on a "1000 point system" or a "2000 point system," but the percentages awarded to specific areas would still remain somewhat the same.

SELECTIONS

The recorder breaks up the board into panels of individuals. Each panel will normally consist of at least one officer and senior/master chiefs from the professional area that they will be screening, i.e., deck, medical/dental, construction, aviation, etc. This means that a Quartermaster would be sitting on the panel that screens QM records, etc. If a particular rating is not represented by a panel member, then a panel member in a closely related rating would screen candidates in that rating.

SELECTION BOARD "SCATTERGRAM"

%	Nr.	Cum.		%	Nr.	Cum.
100	2	2		49	10	536
98	8	10		48	13	549
97	6	16		47	23	572
95	9	25		45	25	597
94	12	37		43	20	617
92	15	52		41	16	633
91	21	73		39	12	645
89	5	78		38	15	660
88	11	89		36	14	674
86	13	102		34	10	684
84	11	113		33	18	702
83	13	126		32	16	718
81	9	135		30	10	728
80	16	151		28	20	748
78	12	163		26	19	767
77	10	173		24	12	779
75	16	189		23	9	788
73	19	208		22	8	796
72	22	230		20	10	806
70	18	248		18	9	815
69	23	271		17	5	820
67	21	292		16	4	824
66	23	315		14	6	830
64	20	335		12	4	834
63	19	354		10	3	837
62	20	374		9	2	839
61	17	391		8	3	842
60	20	411		6	5	847
58	24	435		4	2	849
56	22	457		3	1	850
55	21	478		2	2	852
53	20	798		0	7	859
51	18	516				
50	10	526				

Selection panel members review a folder prepared for each candidate. The folder contains the candidates' microform record, a brief sheet constructed by the board, plus any correspondence concerning the individual received just before or during the period the board is in session. Normally, any correspondence received during the final week of deliberation is not considered.

The panel member assigns numerical scores on the work sheet listing the different areas being considered. A second panel member then "scores" the same individual. Results are compared for consistency. If there is a large difference between the two scores given by the panel members, the candidate's record is re-screened.

SLATING

After the screening and scoring process, the candidates in each rating are "slated," or listed from top to bottom according to their numerical score obtained from the screening. The quota for each rating determines who is above and below the "selected" line of the slate. The panel members at each table must then agree on their list of recommended candidates for promotion.

THE "SCATTERGRAM"

Refer to the chart on the previous page. The scattergram is a tool most - but not all - selection boards use. In the example provided, a "percentage" factor is used to signify a vote of confidence in each service record as reviewed. This scattergram could also be made up using total number of points accumulated in scoring instead of a "percentage." In the example, the CPO board has just finished reviewing all the records for the Boatswain's Mate rating. Each eligible candidate (859 total eligible) has a "percentage factor" assigned.

The scattergram is a convenient display of all these records. The ones with the greatest confidence are listed first. The 1st column is the confidence rating (%), the 2nd is the number of records with that rating, and the 3rd column is the cumulative number of records which have received at least that confidence level. For example, the chart shows that 2 people had a 100% confidence level rating. If you look at the 95% rating, there are 9 records that have received exactly that rating, and there are a total of 25 personnel with at least that cumulative score. If the board president knows that the quota for Boatswain's Mate is

208, he can go to the scattergram and draw a line under the confidence level percentage "73," because that is where the cumulative # of 208 showed up.

ENTIRE BOARD VOTES
After the slating process is complete, the entire board assembles again, and panel members brief all members on each candidate they have selected, explaining why he/she is on the slate for promotion. The board votes on each member's selection and approves every candidate individually.

YOUR RECORD BEFORE THE BOARD
Included here is an example of areas considered by the CPO selection board. You may want to assign your own accomplishments an objective grade and see how you stand. In this section, we will assume the board is working on a "1000 point system," meaning that 1000 points is the maximum "score" a candidate's record folder can be worth. The numbers in parenthesis next to each area title are the representative points allowed out of the 1000 total. The discussion under each major area breaks down the point values to specific traits/accomplishments within that area.

EVALUATION PERFORMANCE MARKS (310 POINTS)
Overall evaluation marks (200 points) for a specified period (normally at least 5 years, or all service in current paygrade) is considered.

The candidate's peer group standing (60 points), and marks assigned to leadership/supervisory areas (50 points) are major points of consideration. It is important to have a peer group ranking (1 of 14, 2 of 10, etc.) in the text of the evaluation.

EVALUATION NARRATIVE (WRITE-UP) (250 POINTS)
Does the write-up agree with the marks assigned? (l00 points) Are the marks too high or too low?

How well did the candidate perform his job? (30 points)

Did the candidate perform in/out of rating in any special assignments, or accept any special challenges and responsibilities? (30 points)

How many people did the candidate supervise and how well did he/she perform as a supervisor? (30 points)

How well did he/she manage day-to-day activities? (30 points)

Does the candidate exhibit good administrative capabilities? (30 points)

POTENTIAL (160 POINTS)
In previous advancements, was the candidate performing up to the new rating standards immediately, or was he/she a slow starter? (30 points)

Is initiative exhibited and documented? (30 points)

Is he/she consistent in day-to-day performance? (30 points)

Does he/she volunteer for projects and extra work in addition to normal evolutions? (20 points)

Is there potential for future special duties, and is there a recommendation for them documented? (20 points)

Is the candidate "most highly recommended" or "highly recommended" in the text of the evaluation? (10 points)

Has the candidate had any problem areas, and if so, has he/she recovered to normal potential? (10 points) "NO problems" is best

Involvement in command/community activities (10 points)

CAREER HISTORY (160 POINTS)
The candidate should display a wide variety of duty stations in career. (50 points) A good sea/shore duty mix, and, if no sea duty was available, overseas/isolated duty is important in this area.

Has the candidate had a wide variety of jobs in career? (40 points) Is there documentation of a leadership position? If no leadership opportunity, has it been balanced by other activities (chairperson for Navy Relief, CFC Campaign, leadership in civic functions, etc.)

Is there evidence of any sea/arduous duty in career? (40 points) How was the performance in such duty?

Does candidate hold any special skills or qualifications? (20 points) Included here would be ESWS, EAWS, Aircrew, OOD, JOOD, Recruiter, Career Counselor, EOD, etc.)

Has candidate had special assignments, such as PEP duty, Embassy duty, White House staff, Major staffs, etc. (10 points)

PERSONAL AWARDS (60 POINTS)
"Personal awards" are those given to the individual, and not to units or commands. PUC, MUC, NUC not normally considered here. Board will award points for awards on seniority basis such as:

Navy Cross	20
Navy Commendation Medal	7
Navy Achievement Medal	5
Good Conduct Medal	3

Etc...

Letters of Commendation and Letters of Appreciation must be mentioned in the evaluation narrative.

EDUCATION (60 POINTS)
Off-duty civilian education can be of important significance in the selection process. (40 points) Boards assign point values according to degree of education, such as:

Masters Degree	40
Bachelors Degree	30
Associates Degree	20

1 Year College Completed   10

College Course Completed   1

Navy schools earn different values according to length, type of school, curriculum difficulty, etc. (10 points)

Navy Correspondence Courses earn values according to "total number," variety, and frequency of completion. (10 points) The board looks at the "whole individual" concept here. Do not attempt to complete 20 courses just before the   board meets if you haven't completed any in the last 5 years. It won't help much!

EXAMINATION SCORE
The exam score is provided to the board for each individual. Many people believe that the exam only gets the candidate to the board, and is not considered after that. But, let's face facts. **It is pretty difficult to overlook**. The exam score is used by many boards as a "point value," and, when used, that value is deducted from other categories to maintain the "1000 point system." In the case of a "tie" at the bottom of the slating list of promotions, the exam score is used in many cases to break the tie.

EXAMPLE OF FACT: When this author made E-7 in the Navy, he had the 9th best score on the CPO exam in his rating (selected as #16 of 200+ on promotion list). When selected to E-8 (#7 of 40+ on promotion list), he had the 5th best score on the advancement exam. **STUDY FOR THE EXAM!**

YOUR "BRAG" SHEET
A common problem throughout the fleet is that once an individual puts on the "khaki," or becomes a division officer, he/she automatically assumes to be an accomplished writer of evaluations. This assumption sometimes ends up hurting the outstanding performers that work for this individual.

In many situations, the fault does not lie entirely with the person writing the evaluation. Often times the supervisor is not entirely informed of what the subordinate did in his job or off duty to further his/her chances for advancement/selection. Evaluations are written on a yearly basis, and many items are forgotten by the time the evaluation hits the Captain's desk.

Everyone has an opportunity to submit information to his/her supervisor to have considered for inclusion in the evaluation. Normally, the NAVPERS 1616/21 (Enlisted Performance Evaluation Report - Individual Input) form is used for this purpose. You should maintain your own log sheet or book with your total annual accomplishments listed on a daily/weekly/monthly basis so that not even you can forget what you have done. For most top performers, the supervisor would be more than glad to include any important information that is submitted for use in the evaluation. **Who better can provide that information than YOU?**

Provided below is a list of accomplishments and categories that you may want included in your "brag sheet." Use it to compare with your own or to **start one today**.

EXAMPLES

* Qualified OOD Inport on ....

* Qualified ESWS (date)

* Correspondence Courses completed

* Qualified 3-M/DC PQS (date)

* Qualified in ....Watchstations.

* Reenlisted (date)

* Had ....#.........(subordinate) personnel advanced during this period

* Received grade of ......on ...... exercise

*Received "OUTSTANDING" on security/zone/safety/admin/personnel/3-M/ material inspection

* Completed .... college credits in....

* Managed to accomplish mission with manning shortage

* Formulated budget and submitted early

* Saved ...$.... on beneficial suggestion

* Originated correspondence (SOPs, instructions, reports)

* Acted as command point of contact for....

* Maintained average work week of .....hours

* Command met special commitment through work of division

* Started new program of instruction in ....

* Acted as command instructor for ....

* Assisted retention team effort by ......

* Provided one-on-one assistance to member experiencing financial/marital/judicial problems

* Member of command sports team (name)

* List of community projects/activities

* Command projects after working hours

* Upgraded material condition of spaces

* Volunteer for CFC, Navy Relief, etc.

* Member of .... Council

* Major deployments/evolutions participated

* Good Conduct Medal awarded ......(date)

* Qualified ...#...personnel in ....

* Personal attention given to ..... project

* List of all collateral duties during year

* Constructed command rough draft of .....

As you can see, this list could go on and on. The important thing to remember is that this is for your benefit. When the time comes for you to submit an input sheet for your evaluation, you will have a ready reference at your finger tips. Complete your "brag sheet" using the information from your log, and submit it to your supervisor/ division officer.

If you want some additional ideas for comments to include, and beneficial information on how to construct a well-written evaluation, look at the advertisements listed in this guide for where to obtain such material.

Smooth sailing and good luck to you on your road to advancement!